SEVEN BUILDINGS

WITH PHOTOGRAPHS BY VALENTIN JECK

ARCHITECTS' AND ARTISTS' HOUSE ON THE ÜETLIBERG

PHOTOGRAPHY
VALENTIN JECK

170 ↗

ZH·1173

RIESBACH HARBOR PAVILION

PHOTOGRAPHY
FUHRIMANN HÄCHLER

176 ↗

HOLIDAY HOUSE ON THE RIGI

PHOTOGRAPHY
VALENTIN JECK

180 ↗

HOUSE IN CENTRAL SWITZERLAND

PHOTOGRAPHY
FUHRIMANN HÄCHLER

184 ↗

EWO
185

MÜLLER GRITSCH HOUSE

PHOTOGRAPHY
VALENTIN JECK

188 ↗

Rücksicht
maxell

PRESENHUBER HOUSE

PHOTOGRAPHY
VALENTIN JECK

192 ↗

WNBA Fan Code of Conduct

you're freezing

you're on fire

CEMETERY BUILDING ERLENBACH

PHOTOGRAPHY
VALENTIN JECK

196 ↗

ANDREAS FUHRIMANN
GABRIELLE HÄCHLER

SEVEN BUILDINGS

WHAT ANCHORS A HOUSE IN ITSELF

WITH CONTRIBUTIONS BY

GABRIELLE HÄCHLER
ANDREAS FUHRIMANN
KURT W. FORSTER
MARIE THERES STAUFFER
GIANNI JETZER
HUBERTUS ADAM

LARS MÜLLER PUBLISHERS

GABRIELLE HÄCHLER
ANDREAS FUHRIMANN

SYNTHESIS AND DISJUNCTURE

I

SENSE AND SENSES

A lot of people refer to the same things; the aspirations are often similar: What can we do differently? We use the privileged framework provided us by our clients—not only the private clients, but also the public ones—to exercise the core discipline of our profession: investigating the specific architectural space in question in order to synthesize new building forms. The fact that the majority of these projects originate with clients who, like ourselves, are at home in the world of art and architecture gives additional impulse to this inquiry.

This broad cultural curiosity creates a form of 'silent knowledge,' which is extended by the intuition acquired through processing experiences and accordingly refines the ability to make quick and coherent architectural judgments. An interest in the paradigmatic social and cultural changes that are mirrored in art and life helps to preserve impartiality and eagerness to discover correlations, while a preoccupation with global contexts enables the pursual differentiated local responses. The term *mondialité*, which represents an important leitmotif for us, stands for a form of global dialogue that, instead of erasing differences through homogeneity, comprehends variety as richness, and nurtures it.[1] The ever-greater interconnectedness of the individual in today's world has also resulted in a counter reaction in a yearning for direct, singular experience and for housing and living space that meets those human needs which are

1 Édouard Glissant, poet and writer from Martinique, established the term "mondialité" as a form of global dialogue and cultural exchange between numerous centers, thus overcoming the distinction of the boundaries between the great continental blocks. See also *Du—Das Kulturmagazin* no. 807 (June 2010), *Kunst im 21. Jahrhundert, kuratiert von Hans Ulrich Obrist*, sect. 3.

locally fixed—thinking, talking, cooking, eating, bathing, showering, sleeping. Cultural consciousness is an essential part of architectural craft, and means, as Wittgenstein expressed it, working on the perception of "the way one sees things"[2]. Ultimately, it is this reflexive effort that determines the social relevance of architecture, because architecture always relates to social reality, even when it explicitly disavows this context.

2 Ludwig Wittgenstein, "Philosophy: Sections 86–93 of the so-called 'Big Typescript' (Catalog Number 213)," in *Philosophical Occasions: 1912–1951*, ed. James Klagge and Alfred Nordmann (Hacket: Indianapolis, 1993), pp. 161–63. The full passage reads: "Work on philosophy is—as work in architecture frequently is—actually more of a kind of work on oneself. On one's own conception. On the way one sees things. (And what one demands of them.)"

That is why it is important to us to be able to adopt varying viewpoints and to adjudicate between them. Architecture is socially relevant when it transcends boundaries and effectively exploits frictions for its own ends. It is only through the conjunction of empiricism and theory—of utopia and practical propositions—that social relevance develops. That is why transcending boundaries is for us a matter of course and a *sine qua non*. By its very nature, architecture spans many disciplines. It is the medium that synthesizes various materials and the expertise of a wide range of specialists (from engineers, carpenters, and urban planners to philosophers), translates them spatially, and integrates them into a whole. The individual components must be selected, handled equivalently, and amalgamated into a new synthesis.

Vertical Village, urban development project, study assignment

II

ARCHITECTURAL LIFE

CONCEPT VERSUS CONTEXT

We are continually engaged with the dialectic process of design, with the conflict between concept and context. Instead of ending in a static state, this process between reality and ideas often results in the formulation of a new, unique, and exact balance—an equilibrium in Jean Baudrillard's sense of "other space" and "an inspiration that runs contrary to any project and any functional dictates" [3]. This expresses the fact that it is not about perfecting a conceptual program, but rather about the life that takes place within a particular architecture and the design of architectural space that focuses on sensuous and practical needs, and therefore explicitly elevates experienced non-perfection and not built dogma to its program.

Architects' and Artists' House under construction

3 Jean Baudrillard, in a speech given on January 8, 1999, in Künstlerhaus Graz at the opening of an exhibition of his own photography, *Im Horizont des Objekts*, which was curated by Peter Weibel, in Weibel, *Architektur: Wahrheit oder Radikalität?* (Literaturverlag Droschl: Graz and Vienna, 1999), p. 15.

The more the contextual influence is minimized, the closer a building comes to being a piece of art that agitates fully divorced from the usual practical constraints of architecture. This can admittedly prove fascinating, but will sooner or later undoubtedly invoke the occupant's indignation. We consider the conflict between concept and context—be it physical or cultural—to be the essence of the design process. The oscillation between theoretical considerations (combined with an unceasing sharpening of sensory perception via the surroundings) and a relaxed attunement to life remains an adventurous and highly demanding balancing act that repeatedly needs to be mastered, and which Denise Scott Brown aptly expressed as follows: "The architect who cares not at all for context is a boor; the one who cares only for context is a bore."[4] We are interested in enlivening the site, invigorating the context, and imparting a dynamic to the structure—namely from a position based on presence and actuality, in such a way that the contextual present and the presence of the architecture we create influence the history of the site.

4 Denise Scott Brown, "Context in Context," in Robert Venturi and Denise Scott Brown, *Architecture as Signs and Systems: For a Mannerist Time* (Belknap Press of Harvard University Press: Cambridge, MA, 2004), ch. 8, p. 177.

Riesbach Harbor Pavilion, photographed by Pipilotti Rist

III

ARCHITECTURAL SPACE

The core of our work revolves around creating livable architecture that meets human needs and has a stimulating effect through calibrated distinctiveness in the built form and manifold visual spatial relationships. "The starting point of a composition," wrote Hans Scharoun, "is the inner structure of a building project, ... the inner correlation of the living mechanisms that are to unfold in the building that is to be planned."[5] A spatial mood is articulated by differentiated room heights and by different spatial proportions, combined with the choice of materials and the color scheme. The aim is to precisely adjust the degree of visual tension in each room, and to connect the individual rooms with each other in a three-dimensional spatial structure.

Living rooms constitute the focal point, the center of a domestic house. Vertical exaggeration, niches, galleries, openings, or internal or external views impart a constantly new and specific spatial choreography to them, which elevates them to exciting everyday living spaces that are a source of constantly changing inspiration. The light that imparts the specific atmosphere to rooms is of central importance. Architectural contrivances can compensate for drawbacks in the lighting (and other drawbacks as well) to such an extent that the original 'deficit' can ultimately be transformed into a spatial advantage.

Double-height kitchen with glazed gallery, Architects' and Artists' House

Living room gallery, Müller Gritsch House

The inspiration for this design principle comes from the spatial imagination of the Baroque. Whereas the architecture that preceded it tended to conceive of building allegorically and one-dimensionally as a function of belief, the Baroque was predicated on a multilateral relationship between man and space. But we also owe a debt to the design impulses we have taken from the urban and architectural concepts of the Orient—for instance Cairo's urban structures, with their labyrinthine alleyways and corresponding domestic buildings with their meticulous and traditionally evolved gradation between private and public spheres. Regardless of the cultural and social undertones associated with them, the domestic houses of the Orient possess spatial qualities that possibly also served Adolf Loos as an inspiration for his *Raumplan*[6] (spatial plan), and which equally have a particular allure for us. Gender relations in this region have led to a spatial interweaving and visual connections in the dwellings that allow women, at least as observers, to take part in social activities.

By contrast, the only extant building by the philosopher Ludwig Wittgenstein (in collaboration with Loos's student Paul Engelmann) can be taken as exemplary for a western, rationalist approach. In this large urban villa for his sister Margarethe Stonborough-Wittgenstein in Vienna, Wittgenstein attempted, in an almost obsessive manner, to translate his *Tractus Logico-Philosophicus*[7] into built material, or in other words he sought to take an a priori, generalizing concept, a global abstract-logical theory, and make it spatially tangible. With grotesque meticulousness, he set about designing every detail—windows, doors, keyholes, handles, radiators, and so on and so forth—according to his strict rationalist concept, but equally to give every façade and wall elevation a symmetrical composition—which, due to the realities of building, obliged him to resort to all sorts of contrivances and tinkering.

Exterior view of the public hall,
Kunsthaus Zurich competition entry

Interior view of the public hall,
Kunsthaus Zurich competition entry

Corner radiator, Wittgenstein House

In the living-room story, Wittgenstein indeed managed to put this approach into effect uncompromisingly, but in the bedroom story he already had to make do with informal solutions. Finally, faced with life's requisites, his attempts to realize the purity of his concept became completely paralyzed, and thus one could say anticipates, in a way, the philosophical stance of his late works. The villa built by Wittgenstein the intellectual wanderer is of interest precisely because it so cogently illustrates the failure of a 'pure' concept—on the one hand shipwrecked on the rocks of material realization, and on the other on the rocks of life. However, this fascinating testimonial to the failure of a built philosophy also elucidates the fact that each individual project requires its own deliberate and tailor-made synthesis of concept and context, of ratio and empiricism. This is an interplay, the equivalent of which in the Hegelian sense would be that between different theses and antitheses, leading to a syntheses—and whose result, in relation to our own work, we accordingly term *synthetic architecture*.

5 Jörg C. Kirschenmann and Eberhard Syring (eds.), *Hans Scharoun: 1893–1972—Die Forderung des Unvollendeten* (Deutsche Verlags-Anstalt: Stuttgart, 1993).
6 Dietrich Worbs, "Der Raumplan im Wohnungsbau von Adolf Loos", in *idem* (ed.), *Adolf Loos 1870-1933: Raumplan – Wohnungsbau* (Akademie der Künste: Berlin, 1983), pp. 64–77.
7 Ludwig Wittgenstein, *Tractatus logico-philosphicus—Logisch-Philosophische Abhandlung* (Suhrkamp Verlag: Frankfurt am Main, 1963).

IV

THE COMPLEXITY OF SIMPLICITY

Entrance hall stairs,
Architects' and Artists' House

Rationalists insist upon the primacy of intellectual concepts, hypotheses, and theories, countered by the empiricists' postulated dominance of perceptual experience, observations, sensory impressions, and the 'given.' We are less interested in the purity of one stance as opposed to the other; the key aspect is to amalgamate the two opposites, and to carefully measure the dosage of one aspect or the other so as to produce differentiation and nuance in the resulting synthesis. The occidental and Eurocentric world view, decisively shaped by Cartesian rationalism, has outlived itself. Both the social and the theoretical parameters in which we live are marked by insecurities and ambiguities. Today's growing complexity and its expected continued increase make the struggles over specific concepts all the more urgent.

Dogmatists—be they Palladians or functionalists—tend to hide behind consequential theories that serve as simplification strategies with which to evade the pressing need to confront complexity.

In our houses, we quintessentially examine how the balancing act between apparently irreconcilable extremes can be mastered. On the one hand, this involves deliberately working with the imperfect and the impure, and on the other, it involves dispensing with any form of historicist or iconic reductionist strategies. We treat understanding the complexity of architecture as a challenge, view the manifold meanings of the contexts as an enrichment, and are fascinated by formal ambiguity. This is because the reflective treatment of contemporary complexity determines the social relevance of architecture. The variables of this architecture—its physical and cultural context, its spatial program, its form and architectural expression, as well as its sensual requirements—are all given equal treatment in the design process for as long as it takes until a spatial synthesis emerges. The combination of economically efficient structures and haptic-sensuous surfaces ultimately enables the realization of low-budget buildings with high-end spatial opulence.

Despite formal differences in the spatial concepts and façade formations, the seven building projects presented in this monograph display marked similarities:

a)

The use of ‘ordinary’ materials, such as raw concrete or large-format plywood panels, stand for an unpretentious yet visually sophisticated and aesthetic concept of materials. This frequent use of raw concrete and plywood is not a dogma, but has come about, on the one hand, as a result of a series of low-budget projects we have been entrusted with, and on the other, from a conviction that spatial quality is by no means merely an issue of the materials employed.

b)

Subtle inflections in the floor plans using occasional deviations from the right angle induce fluid spatial transitions devoid of hectic dynamics. The resulting spatial ambiguities consolidate the apparently simple basic structures and enrich them with new tangible qualities. In this process, the core of the building is usually arranged orthogonally. Plan graphics in the conventional sense are irrelevant to us.

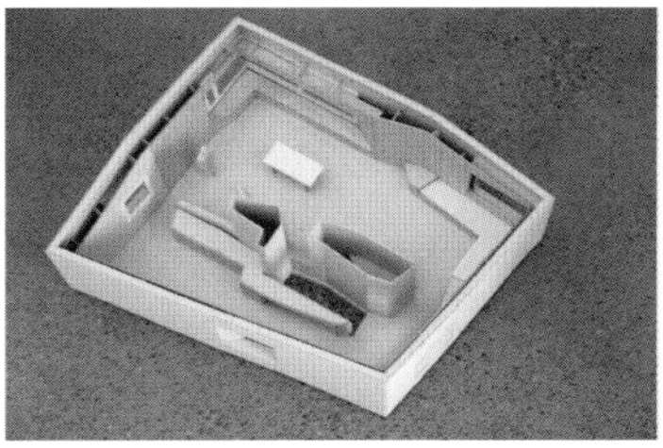

Model of the living room, Presenhuber House

c)

Refinement as contrast: Monochrome or mirrored surfaces, such as glass surfacing in the kitchens or bathrooms, are used selectively to heighten the effect of the 'less valuable' materials through contrast. This concept of materials works in reverse in the cemetery building in Erlenbach, combining treated concrete with walnut paneling and fittings, creates a distinctly solemn and dignified atmosphere corresponding to the function of the building. The intention in this case was to create a ceremonial yet comforting atmosphere for the mourners. In this context it was obvious that it is crucial for the architecture to focus on the mourners' confrontation with the rationally unfathomable, and that the atmospheric aspect resonates with what is a fundamental human yearning.

d)

Stairwell, Architects' and Artists' House

New ornament: We use ornament to generate atmosphere. Having said this, we like to transform the ornamental into the three-dimensional, lending a film-like character to the orchestration of spatial qualities, and animating movement in the space. This effect is created by playing with indentions and protrusions. If the interior space were to be filled like a casting mold, it would produce an object with sculptural character; conversely, the occupants find themselves in a kind of transversable spatial installation. These paradoxical perceptual moments are amplified by the concrete, whose surface tells the history of the construction process, and by the rotary-cut veneers, which have a wallpaper-like, ornamental character. Essentially, with regard to the surfaces we establish a link to the pre-modernist spatial ideas and have never considered the "white cube" as something to be uncritically venerated. Living rooms are not gallery spaces, yet the interplay of art and vibrant wall surfaces is extremely appealing in the private sphere and increases the atmosphere of comfort.

e)

Panorama window, Architects' and Artists' House

Views, perspectives, incidence of light: with the incidence of light, modulated spaces, framed perspectives, and views to the outside, the houses intensify the qualities of everyday life and excite the desire to repeatedly wander through them. Living rooms with windows in panorama format transform views of the outdoors into living pictures —ones that you can also sit in, thus heightening the pleasure. Moreover, expansive walls give the rooms a physical and existential hold, and provide ample space for hanging even large-scale works of art. Innerspatial connections can compensate for a lack of external views. Perforated walls create additional transparency: the space unfolds further, the capacity for multiple interpretations is increased, and opportunities for indirect natural lighting are created.

f)

Plastic façades: Today's construction methods and the technological possibilities that are available no longer necessitate orthogonal floor plans and façades with punched windows. The buildings presented here—all of them freestanding and in rural or parklike surroundings—dispense with the principle of frontality and also with purely repetitive and symmetrical façades. The buildings feature concave and convex recesses that lend plasticity to the building while also spatially defining the exterior space. At the same time, the façade communicates to a certain extent the spatial complexity of the interior, and in the case of multi-dwelling buildings, subtly hints at the diversity of the apartments that enable the interplay of widely differing lifestyles. By superimposing different systems of organization, multifaceted interpretations and visual density are generated. An uninhibited approach to varying proportions, the controlled counterbalancing of the inevitably resulting orthogonal compositions with structural and non-structural openings, as well as the use of everyday materials, such as zinc sheet or wood boards, are ever-repeated factors with widely differing outcomes.

Apartment Houses Hungerberg

V

NON-COLOR AND COLORFULNESS

The idea of a colorless antiquity or colorless classical architecture conforms to the aesthetic thoughts and cognitive ideals of an educated intellectual class, which sees in abstract reason the only true source of human knowledge. This has led to a preference for the abstract line, the colorless drawing, and the clear form, ultimately resulting in the exaggerated excesses of modernistic functionalism. This stands as opposition to the supposedly base human capacity for experience, rooted in sensual colorfulness and the sensations and feelings it excites. Paradoxically, all art from prehistoric times to the nineteenth century was by and large colored. Likewise, the beginnings of Modernism were still characterized by straightforward color concepts. It was heroic Modernism that first introduced radical colorlessness.

Riesbach Harbor Pavilion, photographed by Georg Aerni

As far as our approach is concerned, the discriminating use of color in architecture depends on a particularly thorough differentiation. In our residential buildings, we only apply bold colors to those rooms where the occupants spend less time. In functional buildings or ones with a public function, on the other hand, color can be used in other ways. In the case of the Riesbach Harbor restaurant pavilion or the cemetery building in Erlenbach (both on Lake Zurich and set in park-like surroundings), colors have a constitutive character, becoming an architectural element that reacts in a situational manner to the surroundings. The small building, conceived as a folly along the lines of a baroque garden pavilion, allows the colorfulness of the glazing (and thus the architecture) to blend with the natural surroundings, imparting a Mediterranean lightness to the location. The fragile, colored glass façade that seamlessly envelops the cemetery building in Erlenbach, on the other hand, refers abstractly to ecclesiastical windows (it does so abstractly because the building's non-confessional nature precluded the use of Christian symbols) and constitutes a paradoxical counterweight to the massive concrete roof, which radiates lastingness. The conjunction of sacral building elements, gently flowing spaces, and a modern language of material and form provide a contemporary, countenanced backdrop to the grieving process.

VI

PICTURES IN THE MIND

Roman Signer, *Alpine Hut Blattistafel*, 1998

Collectively we have to accustom ourselves to the fact that, through the advent of steel and concrete construction, architecture has undergone a revolution in the sense of a radical break between two epochs in human history. The one lasted from the beginnings of humanity (from caves, huts, and pile dwellings) into the nineteenth century (in industrial building) or the 1920s (in housing), while the other began subsequently. There are only rudimentary links between the two, because the two epochs are based on diametrical principles: construction developed through workmanship in the former, and planned construction based on industrial prefabrication in the latter, which readily fostered the separation of the design idea.

This process of abstraction first culminated in Conceptual Art, which utterly divorced idea and object from each other. The act of intellectually inventing the 'concept' was the work of the French artist Marcel Duchamp, who in 1917 declared Manhattan a *Gesamtkunstwerk* (total work of art), and derived from this the idea of the *readymade*.[8] For our notion of "synthetic architecture," a confrontation with twentieth-century art is essential. We do not view contemporary art as formal source material from which one picks at will. For us, art constitutes an outstanding possibility to explore fields of perception and ambitions.

The 1960s saw the commencement of a greater interest in context, both in the fine arts and in architecture. Context, in this connection, means the everyday and the forms of social behavior, but also the conditions and ideological underpinnings that lead to the emergence of art and architecture. In their works, contextual artists such as Dan Graham, Vito Acconci, and Gordon Matta-Clark examined everyday behavior and social communication.

8 Serge Stauffer (ed.), *Marcel Duchamp: Interviews und Statements* (Edition Cantz: Ostfildern, 1992), pp. 9 and 44.

Heiner Kielholz and Jakob Nielsen, *Room with a Dalmatian*, 1971. The artists belonged to the Ziegelrain collective in Aarau, a circle with which Fuhrimann and Hächler were closely associated in their youth.

In reaction to the self-referential, abstract, and rarefied stance of Minimal Art (which indeed had its justification, but nevertheless generally had a rather aseptic expression and manifested a loss of sensual quality), fine artists and architects increasingly turned their attention to space as the locus of experience—and this, in turn, altered spatial perception. Space was no longer understood as an abstraction; it was to be brought to life and to be experienced. The relationship between theory and praxis, between understanding and perception, was redefined through the input of performance art and action art, because this approach offered the artists, for the first time, an instrument for sensory spatial perception. Space became articulated and defined by movement. Instead of abstract theses or reflections on art, this corporeal transformation conveyed an intensive, topical sense of space-existence.

Kitchen, Alpine Hut, Blattistafel

Open fireplace, Holiday House on the Rigi

The aesthetic concept of *wabi-sabi* [9] has approximately the same status in Japan as the Greek ideal of beauty and perfection has in the West, albeit the two are diametrically opposed. In the former, it is the imperfect that is considered to be the ultimate perfection of beauty. At first glance, wabi-sabi objects appear plain and artless, their surface textures somewhat rustic and coarse. They have a patina, and bear the imprint of use and age. This gives them a similarity to primitive art, without ever being figurative or symbolic. They are completely impervious to what would commonly be postulated as good taste. The preciousness of such used objects, marked by daily wear, is held in highest reverence. The Arte Povera of the 1960s took up this approach, rooted in Zen Buddhist principles, albeit in a purged adaptation completely free of religious connotations.

For us, architecture is first and foremost a social undertaking—specific living requirements and lifestyles of our clients profoundly determine the design. A work of art is duty-bound to no one, but a house to each and all. Nevertheless, architecture is by no means merely the provision of a service, but instead, it ideally provides existential succor. Moreover, architecture always remains the expression of the events and changes that transfigures a building with the passing of time—just as the pristine zinc façade that once first shone in the light of the sun gives way to a graceful patina.

9 Leonard Koren, *Wabi-Sabi for Artists, Designers, Poets & Philosophers*. (Stone Bridge Press: Berkeley, CA, 1994).

WHAT ANCHORS A HOUSE IN ITSELF

KURT W. FORSTER

The lives of architects Andreas Fuhrimann and Gabrielle Hächler have been shaped by the childhood homes where, even today, family members continue to live in close contact with the worlds of art and architecture. Like pebbles cast into a pool, these homes ripple out into their architectural designs—which are commissioned mainly by artists, collectors, and art dealers—and converge with the clients' own requirements. Such circumstances could conceivably have stifled and constricted them, especially since their forebears—Andreas Fuhrimann's parents were both architects and Gabrielle Hächler's were both sculptors—also included architects, engineers, and artists as well as master craftsmen working in the building trade. Tracing their histories still further back, their families have even more in common, for both have roots in northern Germany and Eastern Europe. Grandfather Hächler was a geologist who studied the fold structure of the Faulhorn group, while the Fuhrimanns leaned more towards mathematics, initially prompting Andreas to study physics for several semesters before eventually focusing entirely on architecture. Another important influence was Andreas's independent-minded mother, Verena Fuhrimann, who was a pioneering figure in the male dominated world of Swiss architects, and who was very supportive of Gabrielle's career choice.

While family traditions such as these may create opportunities and pave the way to a career, the pressures they bring should not be underestimated. Gabrielle Hächler still recalls a sense of ambivalence between home and studio in her younger days—a time of constant new discoveries and excitement, coupled with a somewhat distant relationship to her father. Home and studio were two opposite poles, and a balance had to be found between them. Peter Hächler (1922–1999) had originally considered a career in architecture, but then chose to study sculpture, training with Germaine Richier in Paris. The inherent spatial tension of Richier's sculptures is transposed by Hächler into a more outwardly projected expression of form that is calculated to create a sense of alternating flatness and three-dimensionality: to the eye, they appear mutable, deceptively changing their form even at a distance of only a step or two. Just as an architect can distort and overlap a building form in perspectival views, Hächler preferred working within the visual context of public places and in close association with architecture. He concentrated increasingly on stereometric speculation far beyond its application to abstract sculptures, withdrawing into a world of his own. But the family home always remained a center of social life.

Peter Hächler commissioned the innovative architect Pierre Zoelly (1923–2003),

ARCHITECTURE BETWEEN MOVEMENT AND VISION

who had once been a classmate, to design his house and studio. In 1964, Zoelly's architecture brought a hint of the wider world to the little town of Lenzburg. It was not the rural surroundings, but recent developments in France and the United States that inspired the design of the building, setting sights on a horizon that remains relevant to this day. The client had spent a decade in Paris, and the architect had just returned from a lengthy stay in the United States. Both of them sought to translate that experience demonstratively into the building they created in their Swiss homeland. They did so outstandingly well: the Hächler House was writ large in postwar architecture. It is one of Zoelly's finest works, setting a quasi-brutalist milestone (irreverent as that may sound) in the Swiss architectural landscape, based on two discrete architectural traditions: a deliberately coarse-grained concrete architecture on the one hand and a seemingly traditional rural timber construction on the other, tempered by diagonal transitions and varied window forms. The combination is reminiscent of similar experiments in the USA by Marcel Breuer and Louis Kahn, whereas the concrete architecture of the time in Switzerland, such as that of Walter M. Förderer (1928–2006), tended to avoid combining the two materials, even though wood was widely used as cladding. In the case of the Hächler House, however, it is the combination itself that is the main theme. The contrasting qualities—thermal and material, tactile and acoustic—lend the building a tangible sense of tension.

Fuhrimann's parents, on the other hand, used the structural and aesthetic homogeneity of concrete for a building project on a sloping site in Ennetbaden (Canton Aargau), where they also built their shared home and studio. The studio takes the form of a proscenium, while the residential tract is vertically layered and the stairs are anchored within the layout of the terracing. Growing up in this house, Andreas Fuhrimann must have developed his earliest perceptions of a way of building that combines the prominently exposed position of the house and its interlocked arrangement. The fact that Fuhrimann and Hächler have included images of their childhood homes on their website has little to do with a sense of reverence towards their families, but instead

House and yard

View of the stairwell

Living room

gives an indication of their studio's architectural roots.

What Pierre Zoelly's true achievement is and what influence it has had on our architects will be addressed later. Two aspects of Zoelly's architecture are already engrained in both the Fuhrimann Hächler family history and the regional vernacular: on the one hand, a strong family interest in geology, geometry, and sculpture, and on the other hand, a general characteristic of Swiss architecture. From Robert Maillart and Le Corbusier to Herzog & de Meuron, concrete has been the material of choice—so much so that it has almost become a national hallmark, further underpinned by an industry operating internationally. But there is also a conspicuous sense for timber construction and all its constructive nuances. Thanks to their talent and a keen awareness of the material prerequisites of architecture, Fuhrimann Hächler distilled new opportunities from both building traditions.

In seeking to grasp the essence of Fuhrimann Hächler's buildings, certain aspects come to the fore that have their origin in the building sites and in the interaction of views and access. These may involve seemingly coincidental situations, but they only remotely begin to explain the characteristic traits of these buildings. Mere classifications are equally inadequate, because beyond the common regional circumstances (sloping sites, layout of stairs, materials), it is about fundamentals: What connects a building with its locus without resorting to hackneyed or nebulous concepts? How can a building be anchored within itself without turning a blind eye to its surroundings and the lives of its residents? These are two fundamental questions that need to be considered in ever changing, though by no means arbitrary, forms. If Fuhrimann Hächler's buildings appear particularly compelling on a sloping site, or at least in vertical terms, that is because the vertical organization of their buildings gives form to a condition that links them to erection of the buildings—to their 'upright' nature—and to the tensions that prevail in the world around us. The fact that, at the same time, a distinct correlation between the core and the exterior of the building comes into play may perhaps be due to their tendency to create a kind of bridging effect – by coupling a chimney with a flight of stairs, or creating an unexpected alignment of balcony and corridor—that opens up a sudden insight, changing our way of seeing and undermining our perceptions. This same kind of duality is evident in Zoelly's Hächler House in Lenzburg; Gabrielle Hächler recalls seeking out hiding places and yet still being able to keep in touch with everyone secretly. The house as a whole was never entirely beyond grasp even in such hiding places, and although the building provided the children with ample opportunity to find little places of refuge, at the same time it had an almost disarming simplicity—a rare thing in a time when every inch of space was precious.

It is easy to surmise that the affinity between Pierre Zoelly's architecture and that of Fuhrimann Hächler is not so much one of continuity but of selective detachment. Our architects share the view that a house should always be a whole, the parts of which are connected in a way that is not definitively fixed, but constantly changing in the eyes of the occupant. The fundamental correlation of moving and seeing, of rising and falling, of restraint and release, determines the way the house is perceived and reminds us that the architects want to create a setting for life and not just a place for living. Once you have noticed this quality, which is by no means merely incidental, in one of their houses, you not only start to notice it in others, but can even see how this must have evolved out of their childhood homes. There is nothing passive about this approach; the architects do not take the easy road of simply emulating an existing model. They are not developing their designs on the basis of a legacy, but on the strength of their own talent, taking something already fully formed and hewing from it something altogether new, yet never devoid of memory.

It is worth bearing in mind the circumstances under which Fuhrimann Hächler have interlocked their notions of core and exterior, rise and fall, exposure and insight. In every instance, this interlocking triggers a direct and conscious perception. These are not abstract pairs of concepts, but specific givens that elicit a physical response. Typically, completely unrelated elements are juxtaposed—such as a stairway nestled against a chimney, so that it envelops the static core in movement, or diagonal vistas that open interior spaces both upwards and downwards. The innate tension created in this way is not diminished even in a building with a budget as limited as that of the Müller Gritsch House in Lenzburg. This tension has to act as the coil that transforms the energy of the mainspring into movement. If we imagine that coil in terms of an inner tension expressed in manifest motion, its effect becomes directly tangible within the building itself. In short, the outer shell is perceived as a whole, as an entity whose character is forged by the way the parts interact with one another—for example when a projection meets a view or the spiraling meets the static in such a way that the one is not perceptible without the impact and input of the other. The house takes on the semblance of a stage, without ever being theatrical or ritualistic. Of course, the constraints of a small home do demand certain ritual aspects, such as when a tiny cubbyhole has to function as a vestibule and a fitted kitchen as a workspace. Fuhrimann Hächler, however, manage —even within a confined space and under difficult circumstances—to create an openness that allows the users of the house to follow their own instincts or make a different choice. Yet, remarkably, their architecture is by no means lacking in definition and calculated clarity. This is not achieved in an obvious way, but rather, through subtly evocative transpositions. It is no small wonder that artists and others for whom vision and movement play an important role are drawn to these architects.

There is another aspect of Fuhrimann Hächler's architecture that deserves to be mentioned, not only because it is seldom absent, but also because it occurs in everchanging contexts. It is an aspect that has a physiological appeal, rather than a purely visual one, for it actually causes part of the building to elude our gaze. It is the use of the reflex angle. If the wall of a building (it seems appropriate to speak here in general terms of outside walls, rather than facades) deviates by just a few degrees, or if a corridor shears off slightly, the areas elude our gaze from a fixed standpoint. In other words, it is not clear how or where to go on. This in itself prompts us to walk further inside, or to circle the object whose multi-faceted structures become evident to us only gradually. What, one may ask, is so special about that? Well, these angles may suggest a sequence of spaces, but those spaces are not immediately clear, or at least only partially clear, to the eye.

The house that Andreas Fuhrimann and Gabrielle Hächler share with other artist couples on the slopes of Üetliberg presents itself as a polyhedron, its walls juxtaposed at reflex angles, facing the valley. Its sculptural quality is not evoked by the solidity of its facades and its small apertures, but

Southern view

Garden view

Eastern view

by its wide-angled form. This subtly echoes the sculptural approach of Peter Hächler —not in the form of a quotation or reference, but simply in the treatment of an object, as an observation of form under conditions that are already inherent within it. Walking around the house on Üetliberg, the many-facetted form becomes apparent, as does the vertical structure; there is a height difference of at least one full story between the street level and the garden, from which, in turn, there is a view into a two-story space. On entering, there is an immediate sense of continuity, which includes thermal, visual and acoustic impressions. The massive outward appearance of this boulder on the hillside gives way to a cave-like interior with concrete walls that suddenly makes the metal cladding of the exterior seem like a lightweight shell rather than a solid mass. A lightwell and angled stairway in unfaced shutter-cast concrete further accentuate the rock-like quality of the building, while at the same time providing varied lighting conditions and an enormously flexible layout.

Much the same could be said of almost any sculpture by Peter Hächler. The difference here is that this is a sculpture that can be entered, and lived in, and which therefore has a direct physiological impact, triggering an interaction between seeing and doing, between movement and observation. The house on Üetliberg is a particularly apt benchmark of these qualities because it so clearly demonstrates its contrasts and contradictions: on the side facing the valley, the window frames are set in front of the metal cladding, while at the rear of the building they are inserted into it, while the boarding that divides the glass contrasts with the colored curtains behind the stage-like window areas. Everything points towards a rich complexity, and yet the first impression is one of closed solidity. On the one hand, the sense of tension that permeates every part of the house can be grasped as something that is necessary to create a cohesive whole. On the other hand, the access and the handling of space accommodate a wide range of very different expectations, and do so without in any way diminishing the overall impression of self-containment.

Our reflections on the buildings designed by Fuhrimann Hächler are based on a certain category of building and a certain range of materials, from which a varied overall impression can be formed. Yet there are also some buildings that have to serve a narrowly defined purpose, and which cannot rely on the impact of tension alone. A pavilion in Riesbach on the shores of Lake Zurich, with a compact star-shaped floor plan, takes on a very different air of mutability thanks to its many angles and colored glass panels. If you simply shift the chair you are sitting on, the color spectrum of the pavilion changes. This crystalline object between grassy and paved areas seems to mirror its surroundings, reflecting the changing weather conditions, as it unobtrusively straddles the divide between nature and technology. The same empathetic approach is evident in the way the cemetery building at Erlenbach fits in with its surroundings and yet alters them decisively: the gently angled concrete volume, its glazed areas tempering the solidity of the building on the side facing the lake, opening up to a portico. Beneath the cantilevered roof slab, there is an atmosphere that feels almost archaic, as though evoking some ancient structure conceived solely to hold a sheltering hand over us for some undetermined time. And, as though the place really were indeed in transition from one realm to another, the concrete beams break open to reveal, through hand-deep apertures, the changing light and shadow of the lake. Rarely do such moments occur: moments in which we suddenly take pause, sensing that we are in a place of transition, seclusion and shelter, looking out into the landscape beyond. Yet it is precisely this subtle reference to Peter Hächler's sculpture that helps integrate the landscape itself into the building, in all its enigmatic and stoic silence. Inside, the chambers for the dead are paneled entirely in wood, the grain of which is such that the walls appear to swell, breaking the rigid stasis of the room.

Despite the vast differences between the two pavilions, the lakeside café in Riesbach and the cemetery building in Erlenbach are both single-story functional buildings, intended only for periodic use. Their mere presence, however, calls the act of building itself into question. Why are they there and what does their presence signify above and beyond their usefulness? Without doubt, their design presents a challenge for fundamental understanding. Fuhrimann Hächler have sited them in a way that manifests both their potential duration and their adaptable form. Their innate character is revealed through a state of tension. The architects have chosen materials that, through their juxtaposition and differing effects, create a sense of tension that is further heightened in the interplay with our own physiological and visual experience. It is likely that anyone living in a house designed by Fuhrimann Hächler will not only get to know the architecture better, but also themselves.

MARIE THERES STAUFFER

Fig. A Superstudio, Istogrammi d'architettura, 1969

ON THE BOUNDARIES OF ARCHITECTURE

Those who study the buildings of Andreas Fuhrimann and Gabrielle Hächler are confronted with complex volumes and sequences of spaces that possess a high level of atmospheric intensity. The visitor may, for instance, be fascinated by the sensuality of the effect made by the materials and by the unconventional solutions used in the construction—or by clearly unresolved aspects that are nonchalantly elevated to the status of a quality. That visual art plays an important role in the creative work of both these architects is something that must not immediately strike one, as the sum of what is to be seen is so very clearly architecture. However, each closer look reveals that, at a number of levels, influences from the field of art are always involved. A number of the contexts and effects of this 'trans-boundary way of seeing' are discussed below.

The overlapping of art and architecture in the creative work of Fuhrimann Hächler has been discernible from the time they began working together—and indeed could already be found in projects that they carried out individually or when working under different circumstances.[1] In conversation, Fuhrimann Hächler emphasize that their work is concentrated on the area of architecture, on a way of building that offers variety and agreeable features and also connects spatial quality with technical innovation. A description of this kind sounds

THE ROLE OF ART IN THE BUILDINGS OF FUHRIMANN HÄCHLER

soberly rational and closely related to practice—but, in concrete terms, what form do these relationships to the field of art take? They are revealed, on the one hand, in the numerous projects—planned or carried out—in which art is presented in private living space or in public institutions, and on the other, by the fact that the architects have carried out or are currently working on a considerable number of commissions from curators, gallery owners, collectors, and artists. Many of their clients

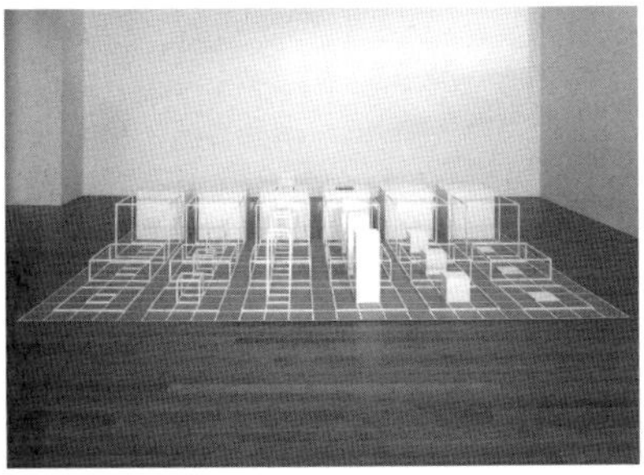

Fig. B Sol LeWitt, *Serial Project No. 1 (ABCD)*, 1966

come from their circle of friends; contacts of this kind are established through the committed interest in modern and contemporary art that Fuhrimann Hächler have long shown. It should be mentioned briefly here that there were and still are artists among the members of the families of both architects.[2] This biographical detail stimulated an interest in the visual arts and made them a part of the architects' lives, and furthermore, motivated a fundamental attentiveness to the entire field of the visual. Fuhrimann Hächler are also interested in graphic design, product design, film, and fashion, as well as in art history and physics.[3]

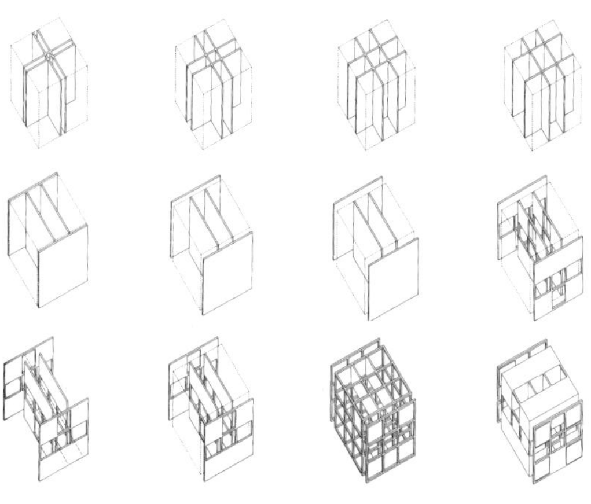

Fig. C Peter Eisenman, Cardboard Architecture: House IV, Diagramm, 1971

CONCEPT AND CONTEXT

Fuhrimann Hächler's sequences of space and the articulation of their building volumes are essentially based on conceptual principles. The systematic examination of certain themes at a formal, material, or constructional level is a phenomenon that has been evident in architecture since the 1960s, with a decided reference to the conceptual art of that time—in this context, one could mention the *Istogrammi d'architettura* Fig. A by Superstudio in Florence, which relate to Sol LeWitt's Modular Structures, for instance *Serial Project No. 1* (1966) Fig. B,[4] or to Peter Eisenman's Cardboard Architecture (from 1967), in which formal elements from the architecture of the Italian Giuseppe Terragni are employed according to specific criteria. Fig. C However, while there are clear formal parallels to LeWitt's modular structures especially in the case of Superstudio's *istogrammi*, though also in Eisenman's Cardboard Architecture, one searches in vain for these in the work of the two Zurich architects. LeWitt's systematic work with three-dimensional forms—the

1 For instance, the spaces of the Kunsthalle in Zurich on the Schöller site (1990, today destroyed), which Fuhrimann remodeled with Christian Karrer, or the bar in Hotel Castell in Zuoz (1997), which Hächler conceived in collaboration with the artist Pipilotti Rist.

2 Both of Hächler's parents studied sculpture, while Fuhrimann's sister and brother-in-law work as artists. Conversations between the author and the architects, May 2010.

3 Hächler initially studied history of art at the University of Zurich. Fuhrimann completed a first degree in physics at the ETH Zurich.

4 Fundamental reflections by Sol LeWitt on 'conception' and 'perception' can be found in his text "Paragraphs on Conceptual Art," in: *Artforum*, 5, no. 10, June 1967, pp. 79–84.

Fig. D Sol LeWitt, *Wall Drawing #588* in the Kunsthalle Bern, 1989

serial combination process using closed and open elements—is an approach that interests Fuhrimann Hächler in terms of the visual results and their perceptual effect. However, in their view, such installations, which are today seen as historical, cannot be directly translated into architecture —especially not at the beginning of the twenty first century, when the task must be to develop a contemporary language. It is much more a matter of confronting specific themes, such as paying regard to materials —exposed concrete, untreated wood, or hardboard, as well as steel, colored glass, or polished stone—that articulate systematic ways of handling and processing; it is far more about specific means of design, such as establishing sequences of views, combinations of differing room heights, or geometries distorted into obtuse angles, which are regularly employed and repeatedly tested in different relationships.[5] The infringement of rules forms a fixed part the system, a process not employed in LeWitt's Modular Structures. Consequently, it is not surprising that Hächler also makes reference to later works by LeWitt that reveal a more playful approach, such as a wall painting Fig. D executed in 1989 in the Kunsthalle Bern.[6]

It was not LeWitt's oeuvre alone but also their study of the work of Donald Judd which helped shape their sensitivity towards the perceptual quality of striking geometric forms. The intense corporeality of Judd's work is manifested equally in the precisely weighted proportions of individual volumes, and in a sequence of similarly shaped cubes, as well as the relationship between color and surface structure, or the space-generating effect that first results by placing an object in a context. Fuhrimann Hächler are not alone in having looked at these and other aspects of Judd's creative work; many of their professional colleagues have also done so. This interest was inspired by the way Judd brings together architecture and art in his studio house in New York as well as in his numerous built interventions and installations in Marfa, Texas → p. 157, Fig. B.

It is well known that Judd insists on elementary geometric forms and the primacy of symmetry. This way of operating with distinct formal boundaries is not found in the buildings of Fuhrimann Hächler. If their buildings increasingly have polygonal shapes, these volumes build on the experience of that striking quality inherent in simplicity, which they continue in a playful way.
The character of an object is always present, whether in the glass pavilion at Riesbach harbor in Zurich, or in their competition entry for the Kunsthaus Zurich.

REINTERPRETATION AND EXTENSION

Fuhrimann Hächler leave the framework of conceptual art in the sense used by LeWitt or Judd at those moments when their work is shaped by a playful infringement of the rules, by a delight in the unconventional, and a fondness for the quirky—factors that led the two architects to examine the work of Richard Artschwager.

Since the 1960s, this American artist has been known in particular for his furniture sculptures whose surfaces are made of Formica. The pattern of the top layer of this laminate often imitates wood grain or stone. On occasions, Artschwager painted the surfaces of such sculptures with imitations of other materials. Their generally simple forms have led critics to link these sculptures to conceptual art and minimal art, while their relationship to everyday objects has also suggested a connection to Pop Art.[7] The uncertainty about which specific art context they should be ascribed to goes hand-in-hand with the unclear status of Artschwager's works which are somewhere between furniture and artwork—you recognize the object presented but cannot always use it. For example, the table sculpture [Fig. E] has legs represented by strips of light-colored laminate, but the dark area of laminate between them prevents you from sitting comfortably at the table. Above and beyond this, in his work Artschwager operates at an interface between sculpture and picture: as a plastic construction, his work has the status of an object, but, at the same time, because of certain measures—like the formal reduction and painted or laminated areas of color, it can be allotted to the realm of the pictorial.

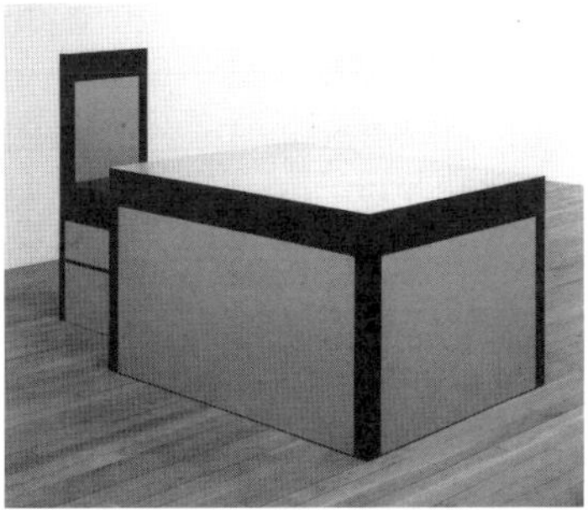

Fig. E Richard Artschwager, *Table and Chair,* 1964

It is this refusal to be unambiguously classified that fascinates Fuhrimann Hächler and that drives them in their own work to see and to think about things in a new way. "The next time we'll do it completely differently," or, "It should be something that is precisely *not* expected"—statements like these are typical of the two architects. Likewise, they share with Artschwager an interest in pictorial qualities,

5 Fuhrimann Hächler's work with different room heights and modulated visual relationships also indicates strong references to architecture and architectural history, for example to the buildings of Adolf Loos, but also to those of Le Corbusier and Brazilian architecture of the late twentieth century. Additionally, they have an interest in the traditional buildings of Islamic cultures in India and Egypt.

6 Gabrielle Hächler in an e-mail to the author, August 9, 2010.

7 There is a direct link between Artschwager and Pop Art in that he did the carpentry work for the installation *Bedroom Ensemble* (1963) by his colleague Claes Oldenburg.

especially of materials. In their own residence at the foot of the Üetliberg, or in the Presenhuber vacation house in Vnà, large areas of common and inexpensive plywood were used. Due to its pronounced grain which is caused by knots and year rings that give it a patchy, irregular appearance, this material is avoided by many of their colleagues. Fuhrimann Hächler see these rampant agglomerates as a quality rather than a defect, viewing them as thousands of tiny pictures that swarm across the surface of the wood.[Fig. F] For similar reasons, the architects prefer concrete walls of lesser quality because the many visible traces of the work processes—the honeycombing around the aggregate, the marks left by distance holders or scribbles by the building workers —can be understood as an additional figurative level and therefore as a visual enrichment.[Fig. G] This not only contributes to the atmospheric intensity mentioned earlier, but at a conceptual level manifests a procedure that dispenses with the control of the concreting process and thus deliberately distances itself from a personal signature. This process not only recalls those conceptual artists who had their wall paintings made by third parties, but also Artschwager's use of Formica laminate, a prefabricated material where the artist can choose the surface patterns but does not create them himself. In addition, Formica, like box plywood, is associated with cheap-

Fig. F Living room, Architects' and Artists' House

Fig. G detail of the base, Architects' and Artists' House

ness, even though Artschwager, like Fuhrimann Hächler, takes great pains with the detailing.[8] Artschwager works deliberately with the idea that 'good taste' requires furniture made of natural materials, whereas Formica is an unacceptable impertinence. "Formica was an insipid rip-off of the fine textures of upper middle-class residential culture, an attempt on the part of petty bourgeois office clerks to better their station.... By removing it from industrialized mass-production and using it instead to make a work of art, Artschwager evokes the paradoxical nature of this highly charged substance. The same is also true of the found furnishings he covered by hand with mock-wood patterns. In combination with rigid geometric forms or with what had once been common utensils, these surfaces trigger a sense of unease, and the viewer is suddenly unsure how to feel about them."[9]

Challenging the standpoint of the viewer is also one of the strategies employed by Fuhrimann Hächler, for example in a loft in the industrial district of Zurich that they converted in 2004. The cool atmosphere contrasts with areas of mosaic in the bathroom and kitchen in a shade of beige, a color that—combined with orange and dark brown—we saw more than enough of in the 1970s. Here, consciously employed by the architects as an ironic quotation in their new context—industrial aesthetic paired with expressive built-in fittings of wood and aubergine-colored synthetic resin—the mosaic walls are transformed into an attractively quirky element. On another, decidedly contemporary level of interpretation, the beige mosaics resemble the pixels of a monitor display inasmuch as the individual tiles of glazed ceramic are applied in an orthogonal grid and differ slightly in shade from each other.

Irony and humor are factors of essential importance for Fuhrimann Hächler, especially in a working environment that often emanates the moral severity of Zwingli's Zurich. And it was probably these factors that awakened their interest in Artschwager. The processes used by the American, always with a wink of the eye, are not only expressed by the fact that he expects collectors to accept materials at odds with what this social group regards as cultured. Humor is also a part of Artschwager's pressed or diagonally-folded 'furniture' in which the question of how they can be used is not asked, along with the question of what incident led to their deformation in the first place.Fig. H

8 In the 1950s, Artschwager had a woodworking studio in New York, in which he made tables, cabinets, and chests of drawers using high quality woods.

9 Kasper König, "40 Jahre Richard Artschwager—Kontinuitäten und Diskontinuitäten, Laudatio for Richard Artschwager on the Occasion of the Award of the Roswitha Haftmann Prize 2007," Roswitha Haftmann Stiftung, Zurich, 2008, published under www.roswithahaftmann-stiftung.com//en/prizewinners/2007_laudatio_ra.htm (accessed September 30, 2010). Hächler attended König's lecture at the award ceremony.

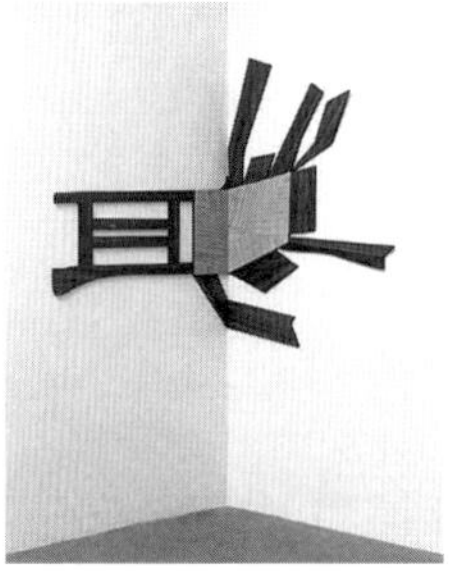

Fig. H Richard Artschwager, *Splatter Chair,* 1992

Deformation or distortion—the polygonal floor plans of Fuhrimann Hächler emerge from this process. Particularly in the architects' glass buildings, it leads to crystalline volumes, for instance, the pavilion in Zurich-Riesbach or the mortuary hall in Erlenbach. Buildings of this kind have a tradition of their own in modern architecture.[10] However, Fuhrimann Hächler's specific method of articulation has also been significantly influenced by their study of Dan Graham's installations. His environments of transparent, partly reflective and opaque glass invite the viewer to enter and offer constantly different perceptual impressions. The act of exploring Graham's works challenges the viewers and presents them as if on a stage in that they are seen by others within the framework of a piece of art—it is both a performance and a visual experiment. For the architect duo from Zurich, performance as a visual artistic dimension is not so important. In contrast, playing with the impressions created by perception—such as views both inward and outward, reflection and transparency, delimitation and expansion—is a subtly employed means of design, which is underscored by color. In this context, it is very interesting that they actually crossed paths with Graham in an earlier commission: an art collector originally intended to use a glass installation by Dan Graham as a connection between two buildings. As the result of a previous collaboration with Fuhrimann Hächler, he commissioned the architects in a second step to provide a clearly architectonic solution. Precisely here the differences between the circumstances of art and those of architecture, to which the artist and the Zurich architects are committed, are revealed with great clarity: whereas Graham developed a reduced object that completely ignored local climatic factors and construction norms, Fuhrimann Hächler built a glass corridor that mastered the complex technical demands with a simple form (2002). Fig. I

To summarize, it can be said that these two Zurich architects neither develop a built form of art nor use quotations from the fields of installations, objects, or paintings in their buildings. Experiences, impressions, and interests from the area of the visual

10 Among the best-known examples is the Glass House (1949) by Philip Johnson in New Canaan, Connecticut, which owed a great debt to Ludwig Mies van der Rohe's Farnsworth House (1945) in Plano, Illinois.

Fig. I Section through passageway, Conversion and Extension Flick

arts can never be directly proven as they are subjected to a transformation process. For Fuhrimann Hächler, modern and contemporary art is an area that they attentively follow and about which they think intensively, fully conscious of the parallels and the differences.

GIANNI JETZER

ON THE PERMEABILITY OF ART AND ARCHITECTURE

Andreas Fuhrimann and Gabrielle Hächler are architects with a great affinity to art. Unlike some of their seasoned colleagues, they are not art collectors, nor do they themselves make art, as did Le Corbusier and many other architects. Their closeness to art is derived instead from their intellectual curiosity. Additionally, their environment has always been an artistic one. (For a description of Hachler's childhood home, see p. 142.) The relationship of both these architects to art is therefore something entirely natural. Artists, art collectors, museum directors, and gallery owners are among their clients and belong to their circle of friends and associates. Furthermore, they often draw on artistic concepts to increase the complexity of their buildings.

The design of Fuhrimann Hächler's Kunstraum (Room for art) in Zumikon, Switzerland, (2000) could hardly be any simpler. It is a pure, jointless form. The walls are made of concrete, as are the ceiling and floor. Precisely cut openings for skylights allow daylight to enter at an angle. The ascetic style of this small building recalls Peter Märkli's museum in Giornico, Switzerland, for the artist Hans Josephsohn. In the Kunstraum, art is treated as something that stands apart— the spatial effect supports the art, yet by no means competes with it. The architecture provides a stage in a subservient manner, offering a kind of peep-show cabinet; as a result, one's attention is increased and one feels an aura of the sacred. It is a small temple for the art collector and his treasures. The building is perceived as staggered cubic volumes; here, the Cartesian grid is the guiding program. Tension is introduced by the asymmetrical arrangement of the skylights, and the window and door openings. The surface of the concrete is itself a kind of drawing, an abstract system made up of the irregular layers of aggregate. In addition, the repetitive pattern of the boards used for the formwork produces an orthogonal pattern.

In the program for the first Kunsthalle in Zurich (1990), the redesign of the exhibition hall is described as follows: "The newly created, well-proportioned spaces provided the calm setting required for art exhibitions." This principle was retained by Fuhrimann Hächler when designing the new Kunsthalle on the Löwenbräu site (1996). Five spaces of different sizes were created that together form a rhythmical sequence. These are simple rooms that satisfy the demands of a "white cube."[1] Since the beginnings of modernism, contemporary art has typically been presented in neutral white surroundings so that the exhibition architecture remains in the background and any interaction between the art and the architecture is kept to a minimum. The only space in the Kunsthalle in which a pro-

nounced design intervention was made is the lobby: the entire length of the wall, including the entrance door, is lined with wood. Long, slit-shaped recesses provide room to display publications. The space is furnished with benches of cast concrete and a massive reception desk. In formal terms, the items of furniture are closely related to Donald Judd's Specific Objects. They are each cast monolithically and dispense with any kind of illusions or metaphor with the exception of one obvious connotation: they refer to Minimal Art, here resurrected in the form of a contemporary design. Interestingly, they do not borrow from Judd's furniture designs, but from the massive concrete elements he placed in the desert near Marfa, Texas.
Fig. A / B

of the western world as a model for living and working. The loft space allowed Judd to try out new methods of displaying art. On the third floor, he had the entire ceiling lined with wooden planks, so that the floor and ceiling reflected each other. The most spartan room in the entire building is the bathroom. Judd also clad this space with wood, and dispensed entirely with a light source—consequently there is no mirror. As a result, the effect of the sound absorbing material can be better experienced physically. A hint of simple mountain life in the big city? [2]

In comparison, the bathroom in Fuhrimann Hächler's Alpine Hut Blattistafel near Gstaad, Switzerland, (1997) is almost luxurious. The renovation employs traditional materials such as native wood and stone

Fig. A Kunsthalle on the Löwenbräu factory site

Fig. B Donald Judd, 15 Works in Concrete, 1980–1987, detail of *Work 14*

Donald Judd's residence and studio in New York's SoHo is a unique witness to this American artist's vision of the design of interior space. For many years, Judd used the five-story building on Spring Street as a kind of laboratory, in which he experimented to find an optimal way of incorporating art into living and working spaces. He opted more for a relaxed form of coexistence rather than a severe, museum-like setting. Judd was one of the co-inventors of the loft, an architectural form that was later successfully exported to the urban centers

from a nearby quarry. However, as in the earlier work, the formal idiom is based on a minimalist vocabulary. Though the ceilings and floors were newly built, they use thick wooden boards and traditional construction methods. The spatial effect is simple, and the use of wood radiates a certain warmth. The local stone was cut into thick slabs and placed against the wall as a cladding

1 Cf. Brian O'Doherty, In der weißen Zelle. Inside the White Cube, Merve, Berlin, 1996.
2 Donald Judd's New York library contains several books on the geology of the Swiss Alps.

for the shower and the kitchen. The concept for cladding the space—combining the contrasting materials of stone and wood to form a spatial unity—is striking. Fig. C / D

The walls in the interior are lined with plywood, the ceilings with three-ply panels."[3] In an urban setting, it is astonishing to encounter spruce used as an internal cladding in combination with concrete. For decades,

Fig. C Alpine Hut Blattistafel, Gstaad

Fig. D Donald Judd, 101 Spring Street, New York City, 4th floor

For the 2003 Venice Biennale, the curators Molly Nesbit and Hans Ulrich Obrist together with the artist Rirkrit Tiravanija assembled a large exhibition with the title Utopia Station. Instead of erecting plasterboard walls, they created a long platform made of plywood, which offered a series of bunk-like spaces for displaying art. In this way, they questioned the presentation format (and consequently the modernist convention) of the "white cube," which had, in recent years, increasingly degenerated into an empty formula. In that same year, Fuhrimann Hächler built their Architects's and Artists's House at the foot of the Üetliberg mountain in Zurich. The clients were Pipilotti Rist and the architects themselves. The interior design of this building continues themes from some of their earlier work. The dominant materials —concrete and spruce wood—are used side by side. "The concrete core forms the 'skeleton' of what is actually a timber building which, through its organic softness, emphasizes the raw quality of the concrete. The ceilings and walls are constructed of pre-fabricated, insulated spruce elements.

wood was regarded as folksy and inappropriate for an urban lifestyle. The native wood is detailed with great precision as if it were an expensive veneer. Fuhrimann Hächler's approach exploits the similarities and differences between the two materials, concrete and wood. The abstract patterns made by aggregate pockets in the concrete and its wooden formwork are echoed by the ornamentation of the knots in the spruce paneling. Walls of colored glass provide a further element. The convex facade means that the spaces are not rectilinear, and it introduces an additional dynamic quality to the interior.

Fuhrimann Hächler's design for the Castell Zuoz Bar in Zuoz, Switzerland, (1997) done in collaboration with the artist Pipilotti Rist, provided valuable experience as a counterpoint to the use of minimalist design in their work. The project was conceived as a heart transplanted into the body of the hotel. It is a sensual installation, a social place that scenographically underlines the function of the bar as both a meeting place and a kind of energy filling-station. Materials were selected that could be used virtually without joints in order to produce a dematerialized appearance. The spatial effect is derived more through psychological rather than architectural means. The boundaries between substances seem to dissolve in the diffused light and color of the space.

stone, and the glazed facades. The use of colored glass in the work of Fuhrimann Hächler has similar aims. Reflections create several overlapping images that additionally intensify the complexity of the spatial effect.
Fig. E / F

Fig. E Conversion Chalet Ariel, Gstaad, 2008

Fig. F Dan Graham, *Heart Pavilion*, 1991

A tendency to dematerialize is also evident in other projects by Fuhrimann Hächler. For a building that connects two chalets in Gstaad, Switzerland, (2002) they designed a black corridor whose surfaces, depending on the light, reflect inside or outside. Transparency and reflections play a confusing game. The American artist Dan Graham, known for his own glass pavilions laid out as reception chambers for the visitor, gives this fine description of Mies van der Rohe's Tugendhat House: "The exterior is drawn into the interior. A free-floating onyx wall divides the front window from the back area of the living room, and you can see the sunset reflected on its surface. It's all about nature. It also has curves, mirror concave columns, very much like my work."[4] Dan Graham has repeatedly described his work as anti-Cartesian. He is more interested in reflections as a way of widening perception than in the transparency of glass. Consequently, in the Tugendhat House, Graham's attention is caught by the reflections in the chromed steel, the

Interestingly, both Donald Judd and Dan Graham have vehemently rejected the use of the term 'sculpture' to describe their work. In seeking to overcome mimesis, they formulated an aspiration to work directly with space, rather than taking the indirect way of using an art object, meaning that they are very close to architecture.[5] The Presenhuber House (2007) in Vnà, Switzerland, is a vacation home. However, the gallery owner, Eva Presenhuber, also uses it as a showroom to present her art wares in a private setting. Exaggerating slightly, one could describe it as a private museum. In contrast to the Kunstraum in Zumikon (2000), the building derives its life from the complexity and sheer eccentricity of the design of its interior. The harmony of concrete and wood is further developed, and exported from the city to the mountains.

3 Project description on the AFGH website: http://www.afgh.ch/index103.htm (accessed August 4, 2010).
4 "Send in the clouds. An interview with Dan Graham," in: Frieze, No. 79, November/December 2003.
5 Dan Graham names the Japanese architect Itsuko Hasegawa as the greatest inspiration for his work.

Instead of the pinewood traditionally used in Alpine regions, here plywood is preferred. The attic space is the highlight of the building. The pitched roof allows the ceiling to be formulated in acute-angled segments. In contrast to Zumikon where the Kunstraum was photographed without artworks, in Vnà the gallery owner's collection is included from the very start. The artworks become an integral part of the building and at places come physically very close to it. One of works from the the Rules series by Angela Bulloch is directly mounted on a ribbon window, immediately changing it into a transparent frieze.

Since the 1960s, the boundary between sculpture and architecture has grown increasingly blurred. In their art interventions, artists such as Donald Judd, Dan Graham, James Turrell, and Gordon Matta-Clark exposed spaces and, through these alterations to the building fabric (often in apartment buildings), introduced playful ways of handling architecture and perception. In the transparent materials, which seem anything but defensive or hostile. As in many other artworks, the title is used as a kind of additional color. Whether the house is really intended for terrorists or this is pure fiction is impossible to say. However, there are clear socio-critical undertones in the artist's statement: "Well, I mean to say, someone who already owns a house doesn't suddenly go out and start throwing bombs around." [6] The loose, sketch-like nature of the pavilion opens up space for thought.

This free approach to the art of building has, without doubt, presented architecture with a challenge and has, to a certain extent, liberated it from the aesthetic dictates of modernism and moved it towards a post-hippie understanding of contemporary domestic culture. Since the 1990s, there has been a greater degree of permeability between art and architecture. Solutions discovered in one discipline are applied to the other in a completely self-evident way. Fig. G / H

Fig. G Harbor Riesbach Pavilion, 2003

Fig. H Thomas Schütte, *Holiday Home for Terrorists*, 2002

1990s, artists such as Jorge Pardo, Thomas Schütte, Rirkrit Tiravanija, and Joep van Lieshout established an artistic form of architecture that focused more on social interaction and experience space rather than functionality. The *Holiday Home for Terrorists* (2002) by Thomas Schütte consists of light-colored wood, chipboard, and colored

The architecture of Fuhrimann Hächler has developed parallel to this movement, starting from an understanding of space that maintained a distance to art, and moving to a complex, dynamic formulation of space that operates within close proximity of art. Their design vocabulary has evolved continuously, now forming a complex system of symbols comprising multiple contradictory levels. Simply stated, the great art of Fuhrimann Hächler lies in putting together concrete and its imperfections, plywood, ribbon windows, colored glass, light, and art to form a single entity with an extremely complex spatial polyphony. The fact that artists like to live in their buildings can be seen as a great compliment. The latest convert is Ugo Rondinone. Fuhrimann Hächler are building him a house in Würen-los, Switzerland, which, with its powerful roof, is somewhat reminiscent of one of Frank Lloyd Wright's Prairie Houses.

6 Thomas Schütte in Munich, Interview Holger Liebs, Süddeutsche Zeitung, June 5, 2009.

HUBERTUS ADAM

HYBRIDIZATIONS IN VARIOUS SENSES

The most public project by architects Andreas Fuhrimann and Gabrielle Hächler is also one of their smallest: the Riesbach Harbor Pavilion in Zurich. It has stood there since 2004, a miniature polygonal building that serves primarily as a shell for various functions: snack bar with take-away service, restaurant, and public toilets. Its surroundings are shaped by the landscape of the shores of Lake Zurich, as well as the villas in Seefeld and nearby artworks such as Henry Moore's *Sheep Piece* or Le Corbusier's Maison de l'Homme. In the summer, the building opens up and allows the paved area immediately outside it to be used as a seating area. In winter, the structure is closed and reduced to the volume of its core. It is a steel frame structure, polygonal in plan, with a facade envelope of transparent and opaque thermal glazing. The irregular form of the building is a response to its various functions; the architects took particular care to avoid the classic distinction between front and rear. This volume, which is visible from different sides, has the appearance of a sculptural, freestanding pavilion. This effect is underlined—and not just at night—by the rapport of colors. Shades of green and brown that seem to have been distilled from the surroundings provide a basic note that is animated by spring-like accents reminiscent of the colors of blossoms.

Perhaps it is significant that the Architects' and Artists' House, which Fuhrimann Hächler built at the foot of the Üetliberg at around the same time as the Harbor Riesbach Pavilion, was initially acclaimed abroad before being discovered by the Swiss architecture press. The two photographs, one with a red sports car and the other with a black sports car, each in front of the angled metal façade, apparently violated Swiss social conventions in which luxury is disguised by means of understatement.

At first glance, one could mistake this building on the periphery of Zurich—which rises up almost like a tower between the Üetliberg and the busy Birmensdorferstrasse—for an oversized single-family house. The large panorama windows that project slightly from the silver-grey façade give the building a luxurious expression. But what initially seems like an off-road vehicle amidst the fleet of Zurich houses is in fact a three-dimensional puzzle that responds

STATEMENTS AGAINST A PETRIFIED ESSENTIALISM

to a tricky situation with tactical skill and sensitivity. Half of the site lies in the agricultural zone of the Üetliberg slope; on the side facing down the valley and towards the city, only a two-story building was permitted. A stream that cuts into the site on the west side further complicated any thoughts of modeling the terrain. Fuhrimann Hächler reacted to the given situation with a compact volume that has two main floors above a garage/basement level and culminates in a roof level with two terraces, which face north and south. One's gaze is attracted equally to the urban surroundings and the rural ambiance—in a building that can be read both as an urban villa and a country house.

From the outside, the interior concept remains almost hidden: four dwelling units are interlocked in such a way that they all profit equally from the advantages of the location, the dual orientations towards the city and the country. All the apartments are reached from a gallery within a common entrance hall. The service core and circulation elements as well as the foundation slab are made of concrete; the other parts of the building are made from prefabricated timber elements clad with a façade of galvanized (and now oxidized) steel panels. Here the intention was not to communicate the sense of something precious, but rather to express a direct and everyday quality, an aim also demonstrated by the use of exposed concrete within the house. Fuhrimann Hächler respond with a blithely relaxed approach to the strenuous efforts made in contemporary architecture to achieve perfection in detailing materials.

With the polygonal form of the volume, the architects overcame the hermetics of the "Swiss Box," all the more so as the precise form conceals an astonishingly protean, almost labyrinthine internal life. The internal staircases lead upwards through a space that resembles a gorge—in this context, the architects refer to the narrow flights of steps found in Italian mountain villages. In the Architects' and Artists' House on the Üetliberg, diversity becomes unity; one could actually speak of hybridization in several senses: with regard to the combination of materials, the load-bearing structure, and the program of spaces.

The same applies in a comparable form to the building that Fuhrimann Hächler built as a combination home and gallery for the

Zurich art dealer Eva Presenhuber in Vnà in Lower Engadine. The sculptural concrete volume is a private vacation home, but it also has a public character. Presenhuber holds semi-public exhibitions in the rooms to which she invites friends and other interested persons. In the post-agrarian transformation of Lower Engadine—as indeed in urban contexts—gallerists are playing a pioneering role. After having established the first art center outside St Moritz—which was, for a long time, the hotspot of the gallery scene in the Swiss canton of Grisons—in the Hotel Castell, the Tschudin Gallery, and the Monica de Cardenas Gallery in Zuoz, the scene is now moving further in a northeast direction. The latest indication of this is the impressive Chasa dal Guvernatur in Sent which was converted by Duri Vital for Gian Enzo Sperone, the New York gallerist of Duri's brother, Not Vital.

Vnà, with just seventy inhabitants, perches four hundred meters above the chief local village, Ramosch, that lies on the valley floor of the Inn River. This village, said to be the sunniest place in Engadine, is only accessible by a road with numerous serpentine curves and has remained relatively intact up to the present day. Nevertheless, Vnà suffers from the effects of a declining population as alpine agriculture offers only a limited income today, and young people are rarely prepared to spend their lives in such a remote place.

The site owned by Eva Presenhuber had never been developed. It lies in the middle of the settled area and is separated by a road from a row of houses and barns that forms the southern edge of the village. Regarding the size of the volume, the architects oriented themselves toward the existing development, thus filling a gap in the village. Their goal was to design a sculptural building that is integrated harmoniously into the village but that does not attempt, in some kind of romantic spirit, to continue local building traditions in a neo-historical way. They chose aerated concrete as the construction material which, on account of the wall thicknesses involved, gives the building a monolithic and monumental air. The windows that are fixed to the inner face of the external wall and have deep splayed reveals, recall historic houses in Engadine. The play of light and shadow heightens the plasticity of the building and contrasts with the windows around the southeast corner which sit flush with the façade, representing more decidedly modern elements. The deformation of the blocky volume can also be interpreted as a reference to the place: by their cantilevered forms, the southwest and southeast corners resemble bay windows.

You enter the building through a perforated wooden door in the largely closed ground floor. From the open vestibule, three steps bring you up to the large multi-purpose room that takes up the entire width of the house and is conceived as a contemporary adaptation of the *Sulèr*, the characteristic through-room in Engadine houses. A further three steps lead to the staircase which brings you up to the private first floor. This is divided into an area oriented towards the valley consisting of three study/bedrooms connected by sliding doors, and the sanitary facilities which are positioned at the back. The spatial system is terminated on the top floor which is presented as an open continuum. The space is dominated by a structuring element in the form of a concrete sculpture which combines the fireplace, stairs, a row of kitchen units, the support to the roof and a bar counter. The ceiling itself is a folded plane and, like the walls on the valley side, is clad with wood; wood is also used for fitting out large areas of the living space and for the sculptural built-in fittings and the furniture. Like in their Architects' and Artists' House on the Üetliberg, Fuhrimann Hächler use concrete and wood in the pursuit of a very specific kind of puritanism that, due to its formal diversity, sculptural formation and expressiveness, cannot really be equated with Swiss minimalism. The bench seat below the large window on the top floor offers a view of the Inn Valley and the alpine landscape.

Fuhrimann Hächler designed another polygonal building at almost the same time in Lenzburg (Canton Aargau) for a pair of artists, Stefan Gritsch and Barbara Müller. It is in the south of the town close to the cemetery in an almost village-like setting. The view takes in the plant beds of a market garden; the site itself was once occupied by a carpenter's workshop. The artists lived for twenty-five years in a workshop that had formed part of this business, and then they decided to sell it. With the proceeds of the sale, they built a studio house that offers more room for their work and stands on an existing basement. The studio house and the workshop form an ensemble that is grouped around a courtyard: the main entrance to the new building is on the south side that faces away from the yard, while the kitchen faces north.

The budget for the building was modest and so, in order to make generously-sized living and workspaces, it was decided to use prefabricated timber elements for the construction. Externally the building was clad with spruce and—where the proximity to the neighboring building required fire protection measures—with Duripanel, a wood cement product; on the interior, Duripanel (around the fireplace) and chipboard were used.

The staircase and fireplace form a core around which the different rooms are organized: the two ateliers—one above the other—on the east side, the large one-and-a-half story living area/hall, and the two bedrooms

—one at same level as the story that opens on to the main space with a gallery, while the other hangs like a swallow's nest from the ceiling in the roof space. This spatial structure has certain similarities to a nearby house that Pierre Zoelly erected between 1964 and 1966 for Gabrielle Hächler's parents.

Sliding doors allow the studio to be separated when necessary, or to be integrated in a framework of spaces that is characterized by openness. The different levels are visually connected with each other. Due not least of all to the materials used, the atmosphere is one of unpretentious informality, exactly what might be desired in a house designed for artists. Here too, the windows are carefully positioned and frame views of the surroundings, whether it be the Staufberg Chapel, Schloss Lenzburg or the central decagon of the canton prison which was erected by Robert Moser between 1860 and 1864 according to the Panopticon principle.

The latest building by Fuhrimann Hächler, a mortuary hall in Erlenbach cemetery on Lake Zurich, can be understood as a synthesis of earlier design approaches. Two wood-lined chambers for the deceased, each containing a catafalque, form the center of the elongated building. It is surrounded by various ancillary spaces—the entrance area, rooms for friends and relatives, a terrace and finally the staff room for cemetery workers. Colored panes of glass separate inside from outside; for some they may recall church windows, but they also bring to mind the colorfulness of the architecture of Luis Barragán. However the richness that the colors seem to promise from the outside gives way on the interior to a subtle character that merely veils the view of the surroundings outside.

The filigree character of the glass is accompanied by the monumental appearance of the concrete roof which continues into the vertical plane as a screen. The equally powerfully-formulated concrete plinth that forms podium at the entrance area responds to the roof. In this area, the roof and podium are connected by two perforated fragments of wall. Are these references to tree trunks and leaves, that is, to the natural setting of the immediate surroundings? Is the intention to add a playful, expressive, and perhaps consoling element to the monumental gesture? Or does the perforation of the walls stand for fragmentation and injury, and is therefore to be understood as a memento mori?

Here, where the focus is on the Last Things, the baroque approach of Fuhrimann Hächler is more clearly revealed than in some of their other buildings. Unequivocality is replaced by ambiguity without drifting into arbitrariness: orthogonality and expressiveness engage each other to form an alliance, which could offer a way out of the petrified essentialism that characterizes contemporary Swiss building—an architecture that, cast in concrete, is based on a rigid stereometry of archetypical bodies.

This leads to a new use of powerfully pictorial forms which, however—unlike in the era of postmodernism—are not to be understood as superficial quotations but preserve their independence. Borrowing a term from literature theorist Roman Ingarden, one could speak here of *Unbestimmtheitsstellen* (places or points of indeterminacy) that are also necessary for architecture to exert an effect. According to Ingarden, indeterminacy is of central importance for the effect of literary artworks; it is the indeterminate passages in a work that first allow its 'concretization' in the reception by the observer. In architecture, too, there is a need for elements of this kind, which allow individual appropriation by the users; they are the synapses between architecture and the reality of life.

SEVEN BUILDINGS

ARCHITECTS' AND ARTISTS' HOUSE ON THE ÜETLIBERG

2002–2003

ZURICH

2 ↗

The goal in designing the multi-unit apartment building at the foot of the Üetliberg was to create reasonably priced residential space with high standards of living comfort for four differently-sized parties. In the process, each party was to profit as much as possible from the 3,000 m² south-facing property, on the one hand, and on the other hand, from the north-facing view out over the city. This resulted in an unconventional and complex internal organization for the building. One double-height entrance hall provides access to all four apartments, each of which has one or two stories accessed via an internal staircase. Essentially, two duplex apartments and two single-level rooftop apartments are intertwined such that the four-sided orientation of the freestanding building is fully exploited.

The intention of the clients was to erect a low-budget building, which was consciously underscored by the choice of materials. Commonplace and unrefined materials such as concrete, timber, wood, and galvanized steel were chosen, enlivening each other in combination. The precise installation of colorful kitchen units with reflective glass surfacing and the extensive colored glass cladding of the bathroom walls contrast with the coarse concrete and the organic patterns of the wood.

The concrete core constitutes the 'skeleton' of the essentially wooden structure, the organic softness of which heightens the rawness of the concrete. The ceilings and walls consist of prefabricated, insulated wood elements made of spruce. Today's technology enables the successful application of prefabrication techniques to complex spatial structures and polygonal geometry.

NORTH

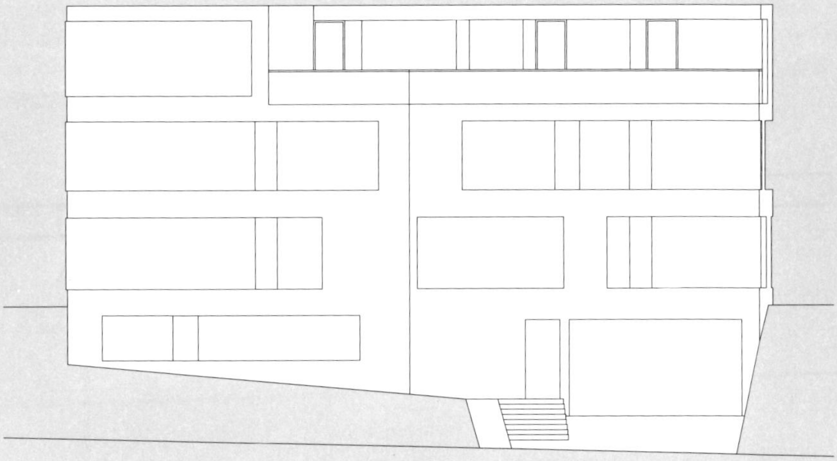

EAST

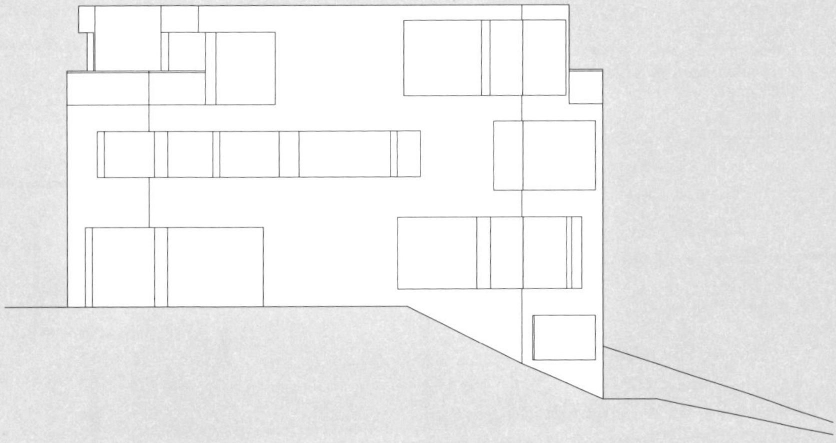

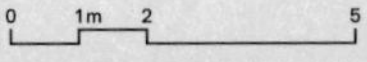

GROUND FLOOR

1 Dining / cooking
2 Living
3 Entrance hall
4 Studio
5 Cloakroom
6 Lavatory

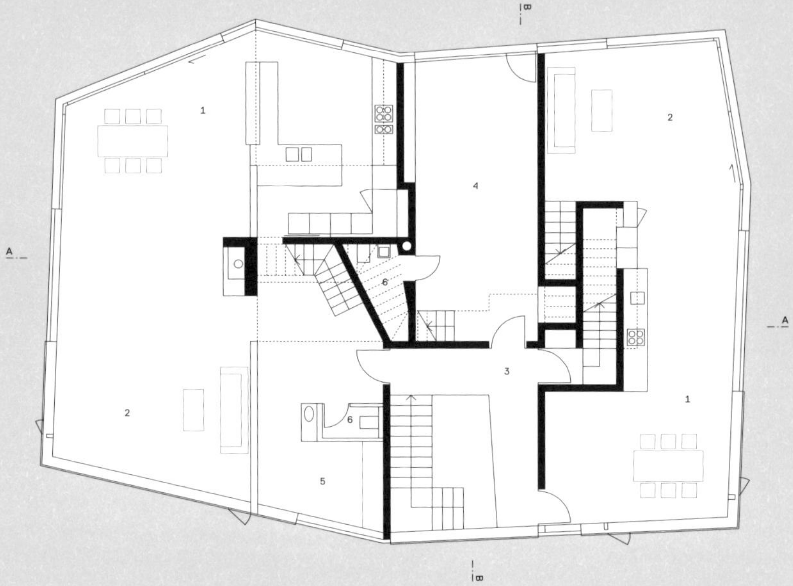

ENTRANCE STORY

1 Garage
2 Entrance hall
3 Office
4 Civil defense shelter
5 Cellar area
6 Storage
7 Lavatory

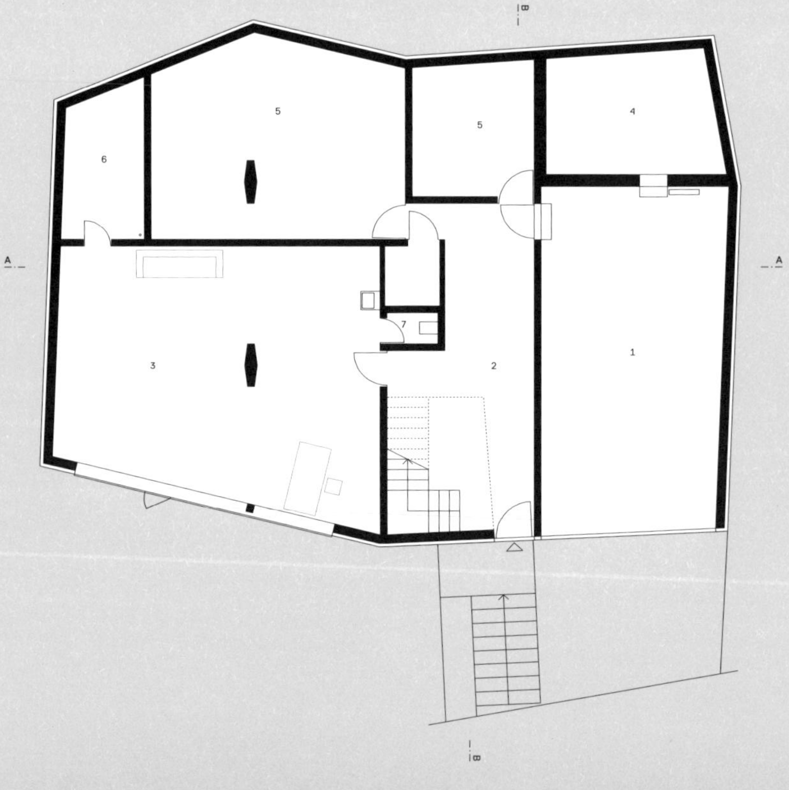

ROOF STORY

1 Sleeping
2 Living
3 Dining / cooking
4 Bath / lavatory
5 Shower / lavatory

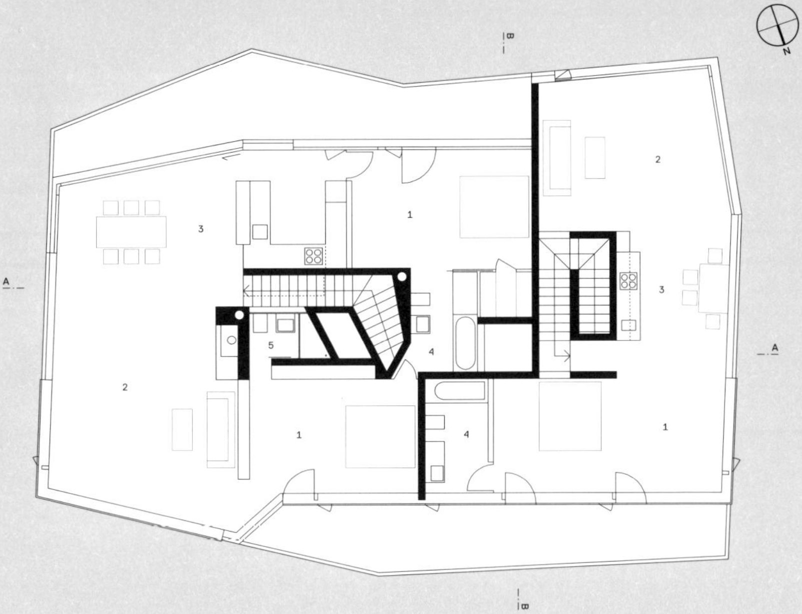

UPPER FLOOR

1 Sleeping
2 Studio
3 Bath / lavatory
4 Shower / lavatory
5 Kitchen air space

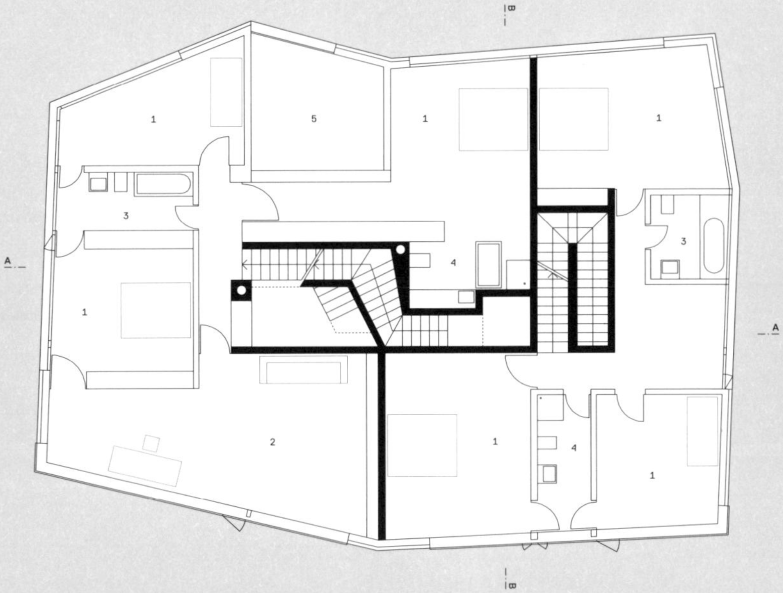

0 1m 2 5

LONGITUDINAL SECTION A-A

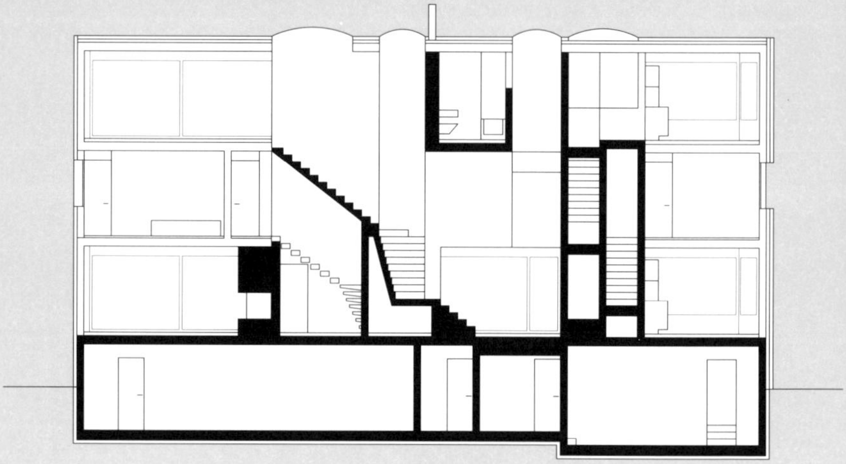

CROSS SECTION B-B

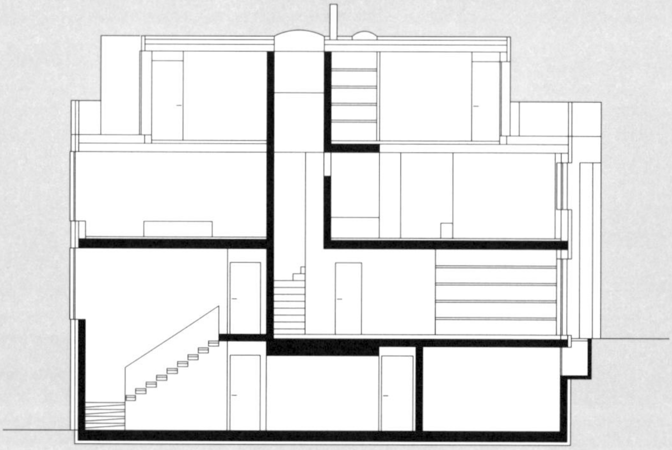

RIESBACH HARBOR PAVILION

2001–2003

ZURICH

22 ↗

The pavilion is an object, set between trees, that incorporates itself into the heterogeneous landscape of the landmarked park. The neighboring Sheep Piece sculpture by Henry Moore and Le Corbusier's nearby Maison de l'Homme are important reference points. Both are freeform sculptural objects that give structure to the space of the park. The modular, lightweight construction of the pavilion follows a similar approach. The steel skeleton forms a simple frame that allows the functions (a restaurant / snack bar and public toilets) to be combined freely. The relatively small space of the quay offers potentials articulated in the pavilion's oscillation between sculpture and architecture. The result is a building volume that dispenses with the usual differentiation between primary and secondary façades, instead forming a unified rhythmic theme of alternating colors using large-format, transparent and semi-opaque glass surfaces. Due to the polygonal plan form, connections to the exterior space are established by the simplest of means. The concave shape of the façade emphasizes the main entrance to the kiosk and the exterior terrace, used in the summer for restaurant seating, and opens to the lake and the passers-by along the promenade.

The intensity and opaqueness of the colors correspond to the requirements of the various interior spaces. The colorfulness of the façade allows the pavilion to integrate naturally into the park surroundings and its artistic forcefulness sharpens an appreciation for the park's beauty and vulnerability. At night, the colorfully illuminated pavilion in the park becomes an added attraction for everyone passing by.

NORTHEAST

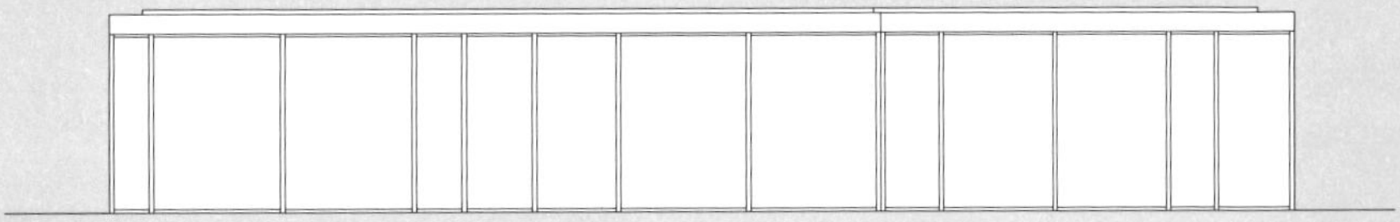

SOUTH

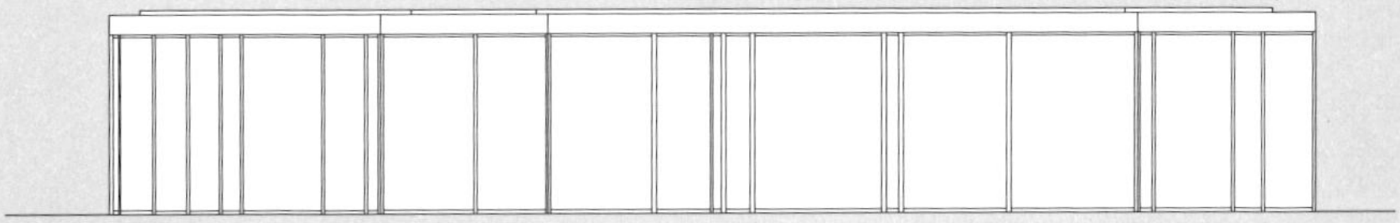

WEST

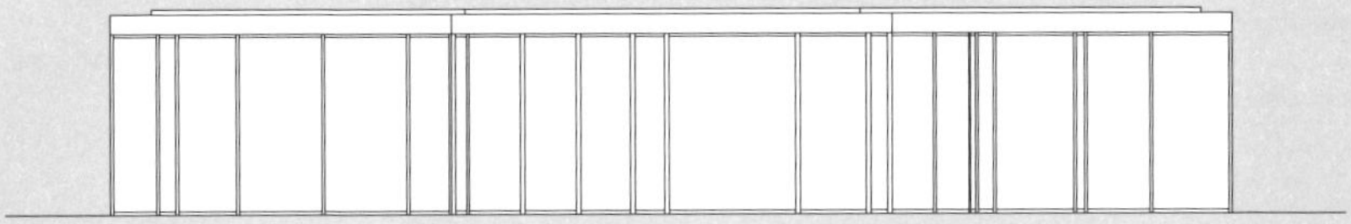

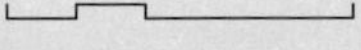

LONGITUDINAL SECTION A-A

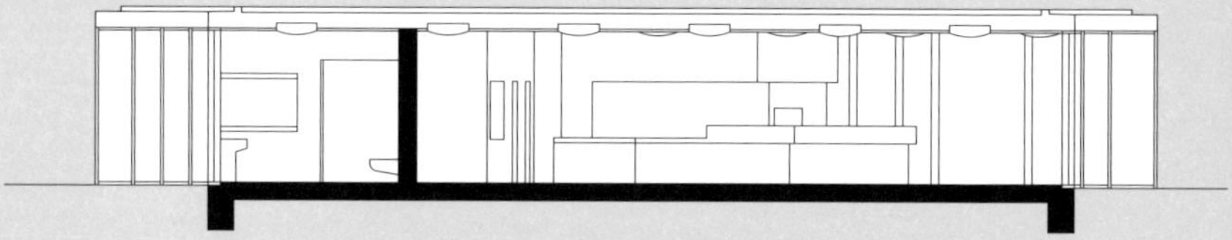

GROUND FLOOR

1 Seating area
2 Kitchen
3 Dish-washing station
4 Refrigerated storage
5 Storage
6 Service installations
7 Staffroom
8 Men's lavatory
9 Disabled lavatory
10 Women's lavatory

HOLIDAY HOUSE ON THE RIGI

2003–2004

RIGI–SCHEIDEGG

34 ↗

The building is anchored to the sloping terrain by a concrete cellar. Resting on this pedestal is a wooden volume with a form reminiscent of a ship. The volume cantilevers greatly toward the east, creating the covered, shielded entrance necessary in the mountains. The concrete chimney of the fireplace rises like a mast from the cellar and, together with a concrete wall, forms the backbone bracing the building. Behind this, two single-flight stairs connect the three stories. On the ground floor, a large living room with various ceiling heights stretches out over two different levels. With its deliberately very low ceiling, the area containing the kitchen indeed creates a spatial feeling similar to that experienced in the low-ceilinged parlors found in mountain huts. By contrast, the five-meter-wide, fixed-glass panorama window that frames the breathtaking view like a picture creates a feeling of contemporary modernity. The polygonal plan form enables a differentiated spatial arrangement and lends a particular emphasis to the fireplace at the widest point in the room.

SOUTHEAST

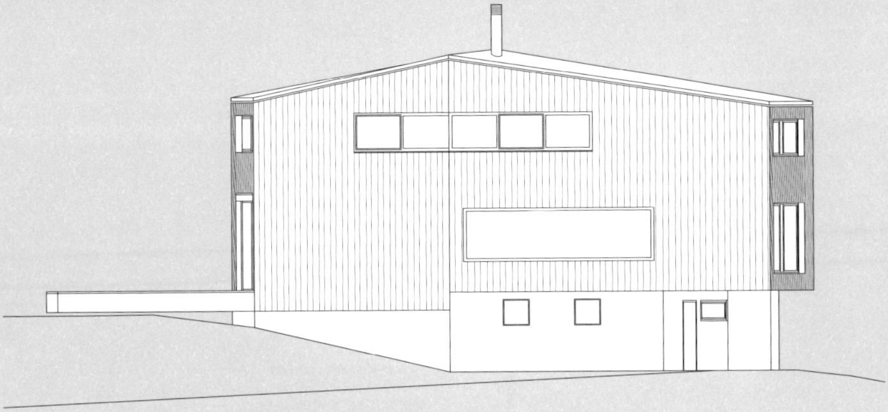

NORTHEAST

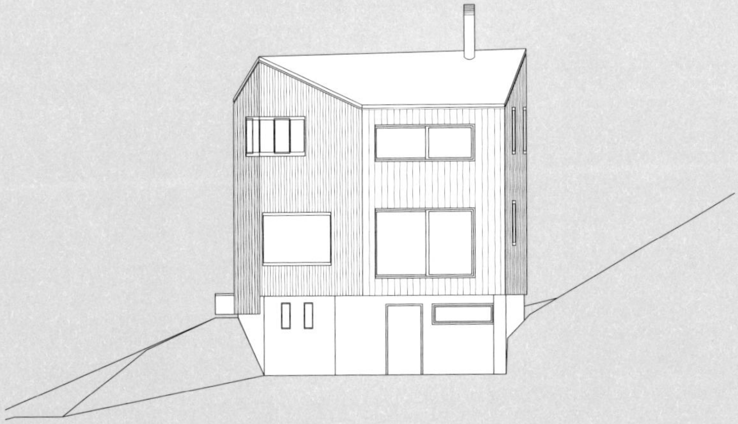

SOUTHWEST

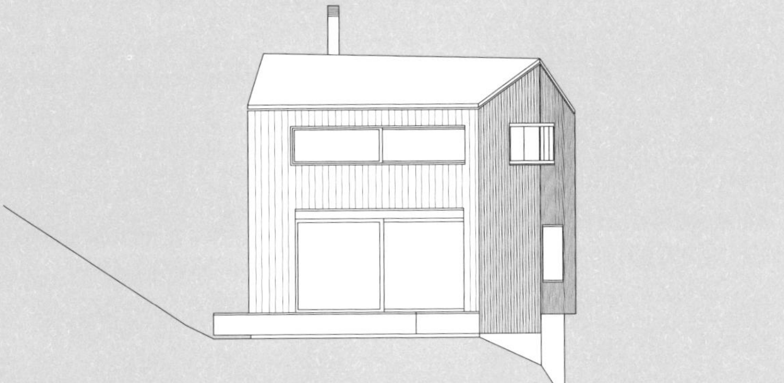

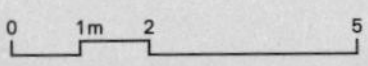

LONGITUDINAL SECTION A-A

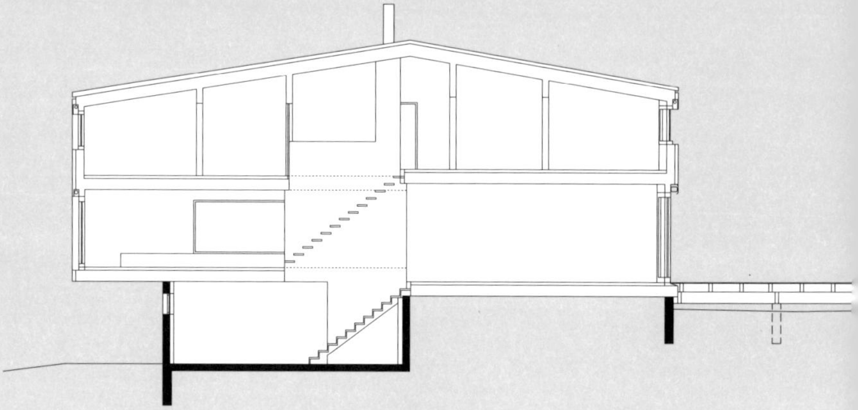

CROSS SECTION B-B

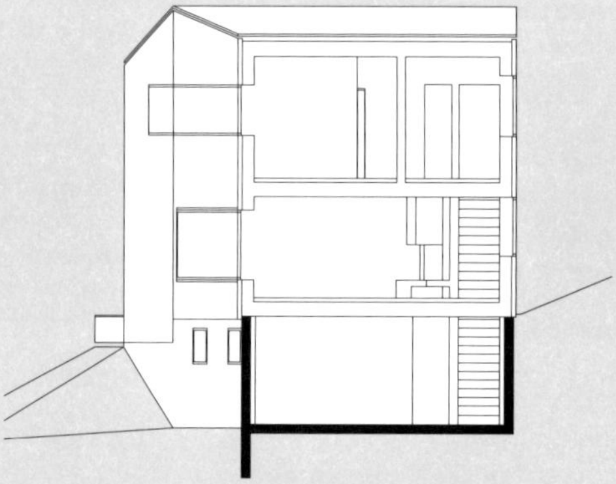

UPPER FLOOR

1 Sleeping
2 Bath / lavatory
3 Shower / lavatory

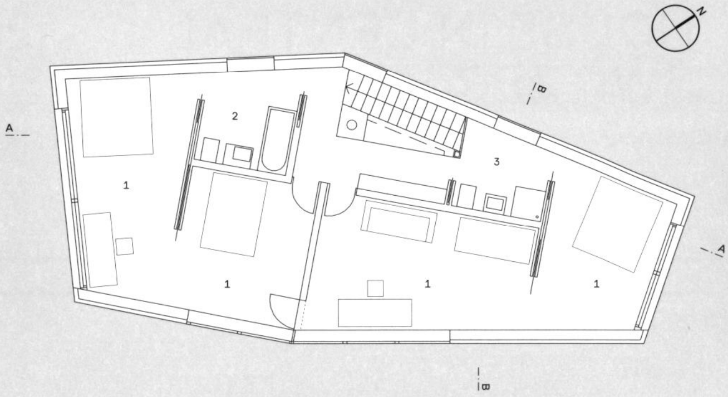

GROUND FLOOR

1 Terrace
2 Living
3 Dining / cooking

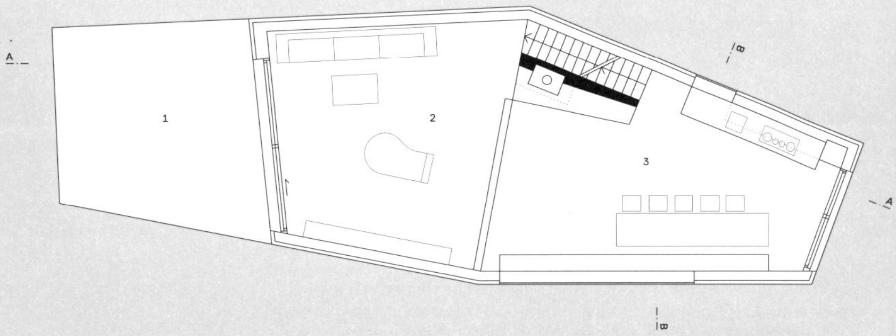

ENTRANCE STORY

1 Entrance area
2 Storage / service installations

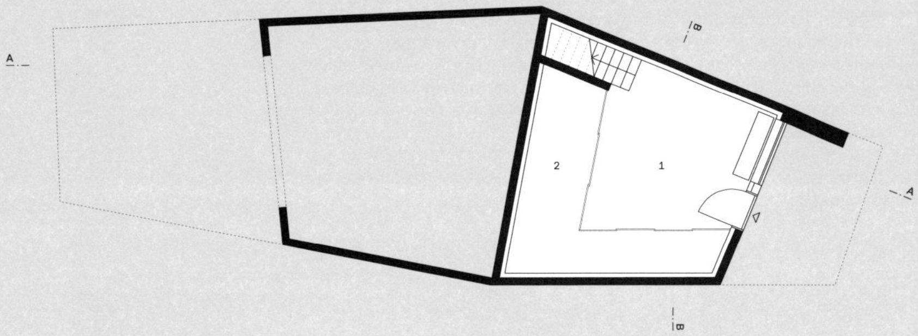

0 1m 2 5

HOUSE IN CENTRAL SWITZERLAND

2008–2009

ENGELBERG

50 ↗

The apartment house perches on a steep slope on the edge of the village of Engelberg in central Switzerland, which, due to its impressive mountain panorama, has grown over the past 150 years to become an attractive spa. The building's concept situates it between the poles of the traditional and the contemporary. The expansive and greatly cantilevered terrace, with its powerful beams, links the building to the Modern tradition. Moreover, it creates the outside space needed for the living areas, which could only have been created so generously in this manner due to the steep slope. From the living room, the deep cantilever of the terrace also hides the neighboring buildings below from view, focusing the vista on the mountain scenery.

The prefabricated modular polygonal wooden house contrasts with the austereness of the terrace, and consists of a spatial continuum that unfolds over two stories. The partially double-height living room is the focal point of the house, its two floors connected via an open gallery. The double-story nature is dramatized by the concrete chimney of the fireplace, whilst the endpoint of the spatial development is marked by a skylight. The differing room heights create a varied play of spatial effects. The library has the lowest ceiling and is slightly raised in relation to the living room. It is entirely paneled with plywood, and forms a niche that serves as a secluded retreat.

The fascinating, animated surface of the clapboard siding of the façade echoes those of old wooden sheds, and anchors the building in the architectural tradition of local farms.

EAST

SOUTH

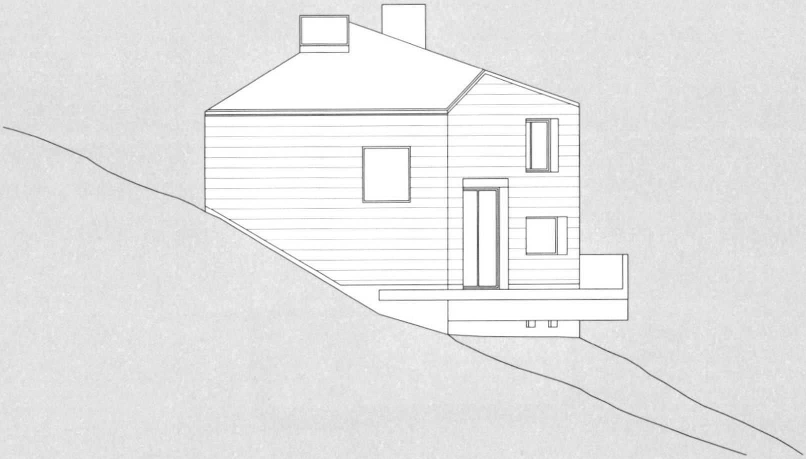

WEST

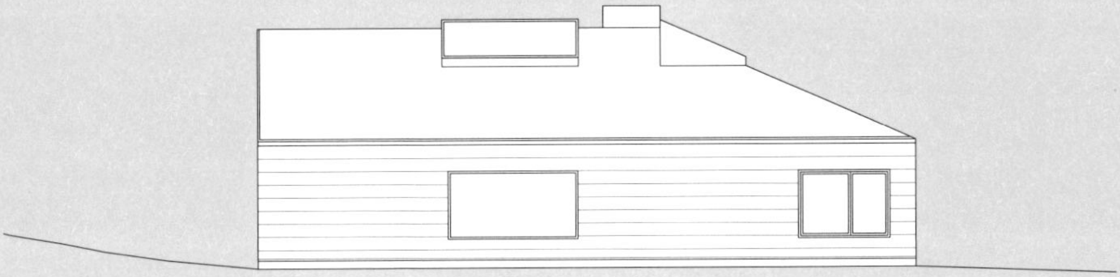

0 1m 2 5

LONGITUDINAL SECTION A-A

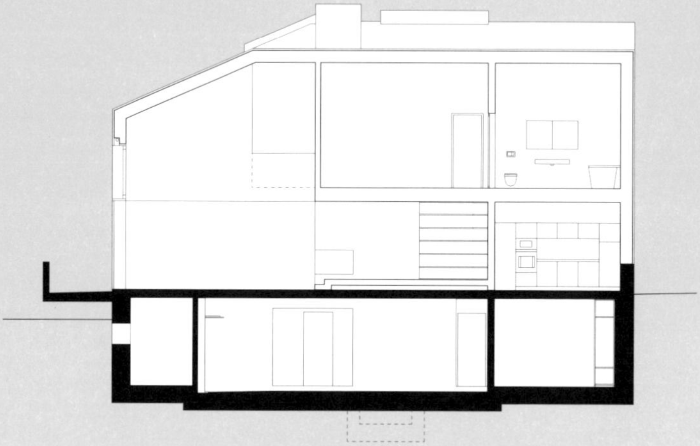

CROSS SECTION B-B

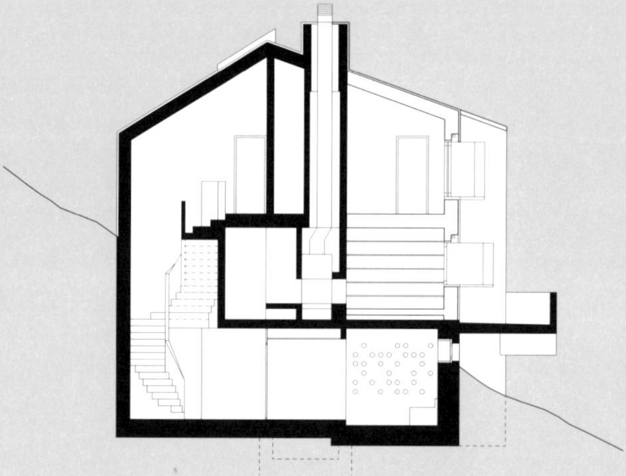

CROSS SECTION C-C

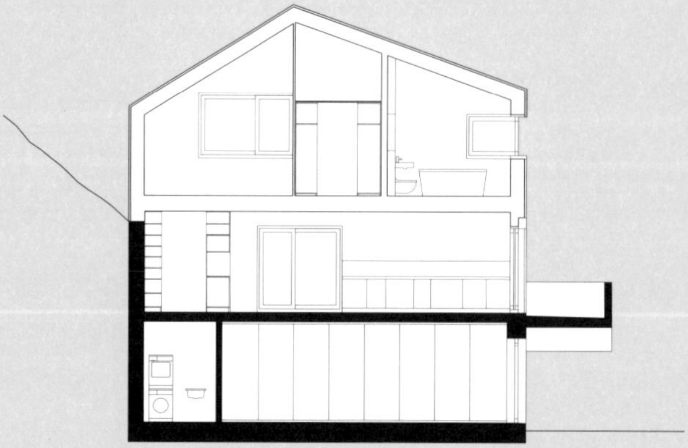

UPPER FLOOR

1 Guestroom
2 Living-room air space
3 Sleeping
4 Bath / lavatory
5 Dressing room
6 Shower / lavatory

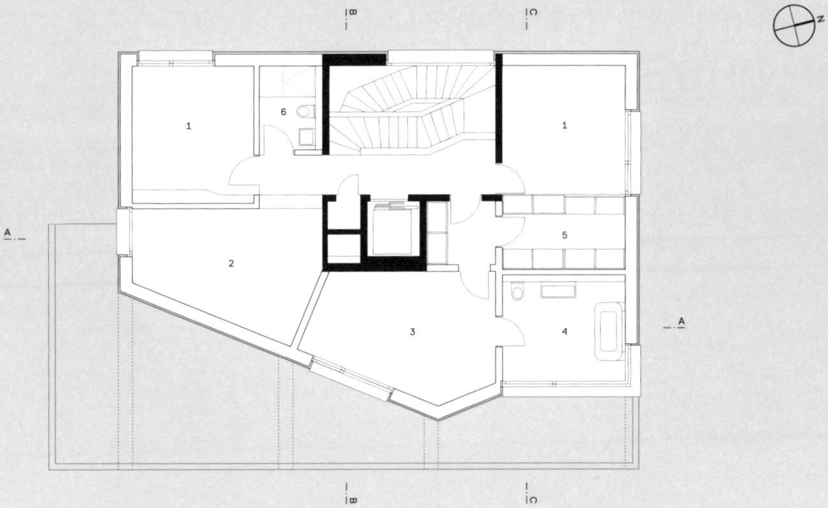

GROUND FLOOR

1 Living
2 Library
3 Dining / cooking
4 Larder
5 Lavatory

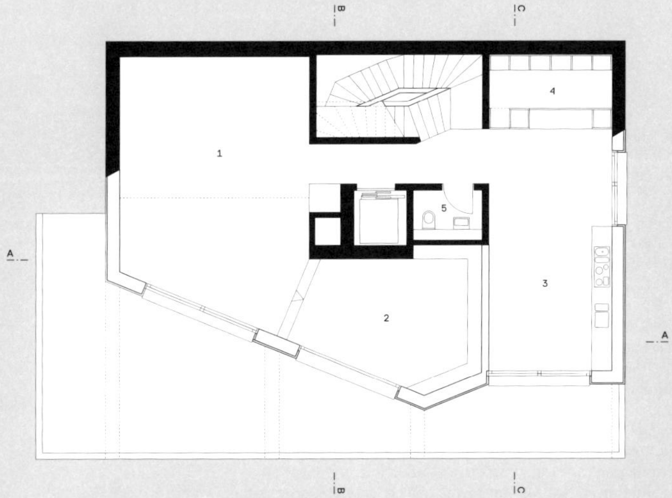

BASEMENT

1 Entrance / cloakroom
2 Laundry
3 Lavatory
4 Wellness
5 Sauna
6 Cellar
7 Service installations

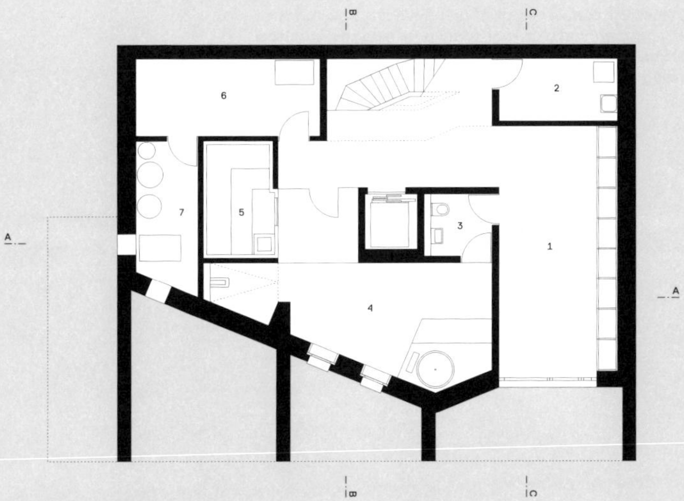

0 1m 2 5

MÜLLER GRITSCH HOUSE

2005–2007

LENZBURG

68 ↗

The search for innovative solutions for this apartment and studio building was not motivated merely by cost constraints. The resulting architecture deliberately mirrors a conscious attitude of life that spurns the polished superfluity so deeply ingrained in contemporary lifestyles, and attempts instead to address more substantive issues. The design affords the artists, who spend much of their time at home, spatial variety and complexity, encouraging its occupants to continually explore it anew. In this sense, the house constitutes an introverted vessel, complementing the artistic work of its owners whilst also creating precise links to the outside world.
In urbanistic terms, the polygonal volume and the adjoining carpenter's workshop form a courtyard around which the studios and the kitchen are oriented. The living room has tall windows that provide places to sit, creating a vivid link with the lush garden. The one-and-a-half-story living room constitutes the spatial center of gravity of the house, with all of the rooms arranged around a central core containing the fireplace and the staircase. The house is conceived as a spatial continuum, enabling a wide variety of spatial relations.

NORTH

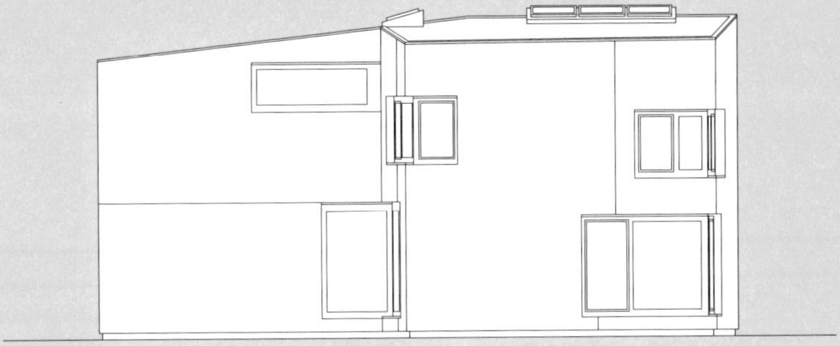

SOUTH

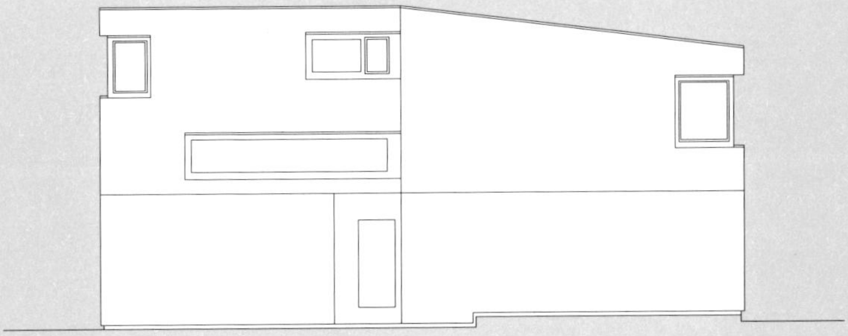

EAST

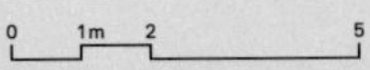

LONGITUDINAL SECTION A-A

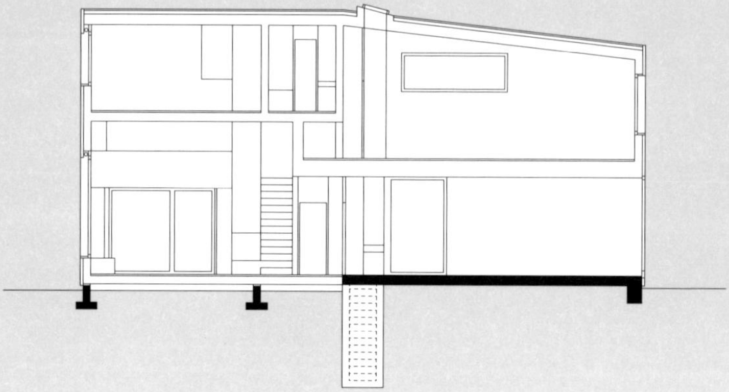

CROSS SECTION B-B

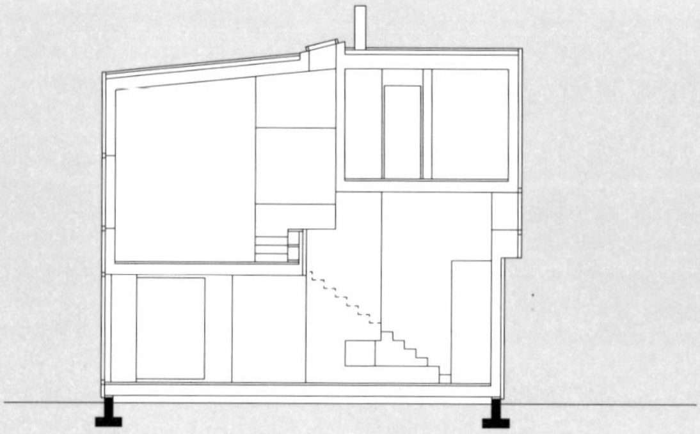

CROSS SECTION C-C

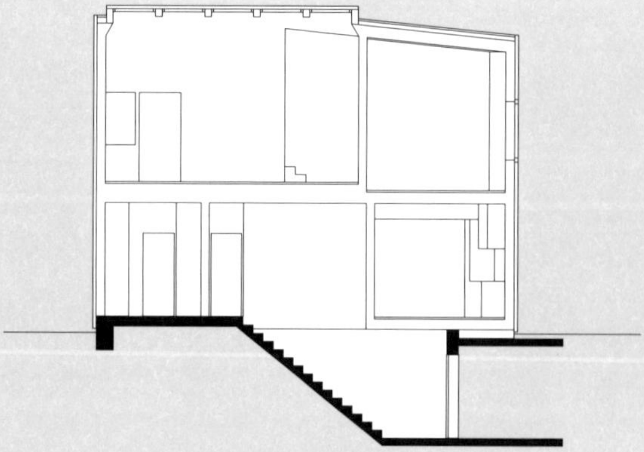

ROOF STORY

1 Sleeping
2 Bath / lavatory
3 Studio air space
4 Bedroom air space
5 Gallery air space

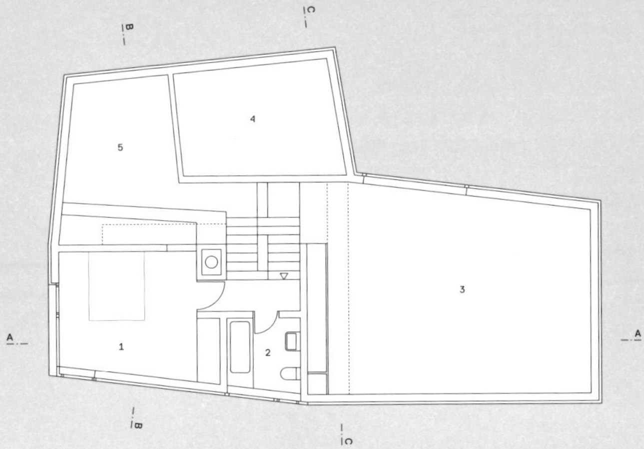

UPPER FLOOR

1 Gallery
2 Sleeping
3 Studio
4 Living-room air space

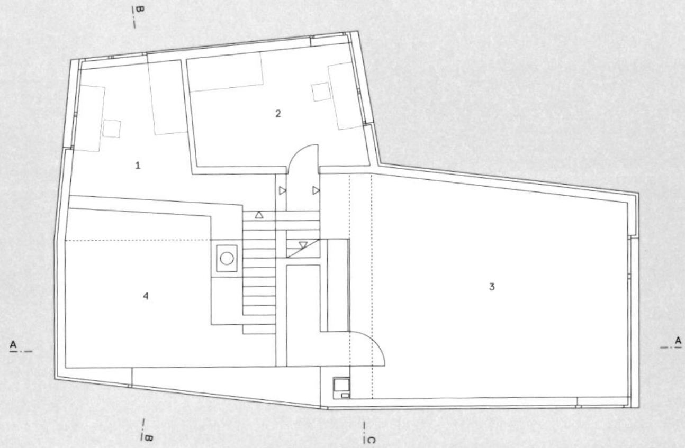

GROUND FLOOR

1 Living
2 Dining / cooking
3 Studio
4 Shower / lavatory
5 Cellar entrance

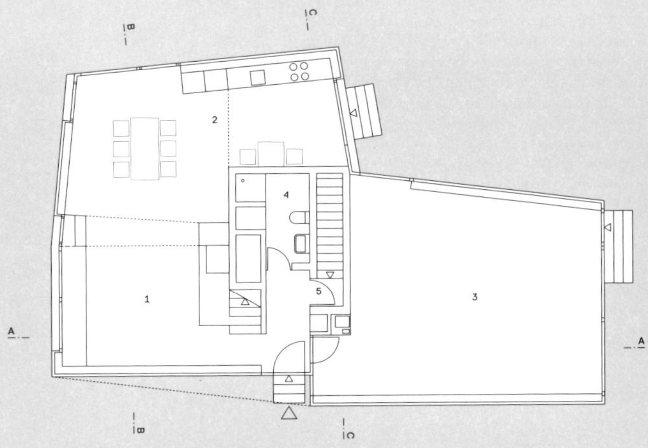

PRESENHUBER HOUSE

2006–2007

VNÀ

84 ↗

The vacation house is located in the middle of the village of Vnà in the Lower Engadine Valley. The village, with its seventy or so inhabitants, is nestled in a secluded tributary valley and possesses a relatively intact structure, untouched by modern development. The particular challenge of the project was to bridge the divide between the old-world charm of the village and the contemporary spirit to be embodied in the vacation house for an internationally successful art gallery owner. The aim was to develop a language that has proximity to traditional Engadine architecture, yet is immediately recognizable as contemporary architecture rather than being conservatively romantic.

In urbanistic terms, the building closes a long-standing gap in the village and the dimensions of the house correspond to those of the surrounding buildings. The area has been repeatedly hit by fires in the past, meaning that many of the original timber houses disappeared over time, making stone houses characteristic for the village. The use of concrete as the main construction material pays honor to this stone character. Only the inner walls and ceilings of the living room and bedrooms are lined in plywood paneling to give the rooms a sense of warmth and comfort, and as to approximate the traditional feeling associated with a mountain dwelling.

The living room is situated on the top floor under a multi-angled pitched roof. A concrete element containing the fireplace and the kitchen gives structure to the space and supports the roof. The over-dimensioned bay window is conceived as a window seat and captures the mountain scenery in a panorama.

The sculptural volume of the building unifies traditional and modern elements into a single entity. The interplay between simplicity, rural straightforwardness, contemporary comfort, and architectural sophistication lends the house a very specific character, which pays respect to the village without being obsequious.

EAST

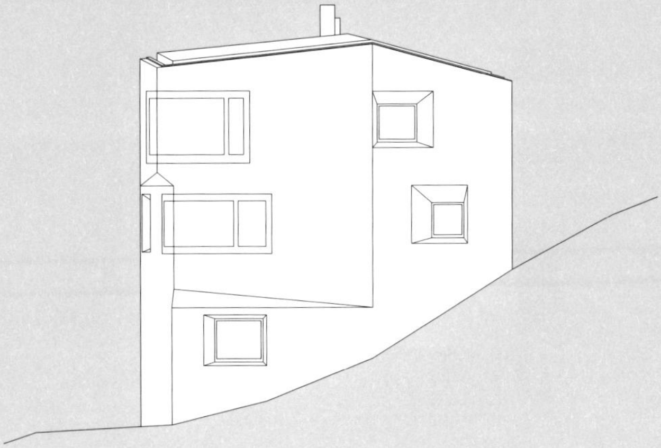

WEST

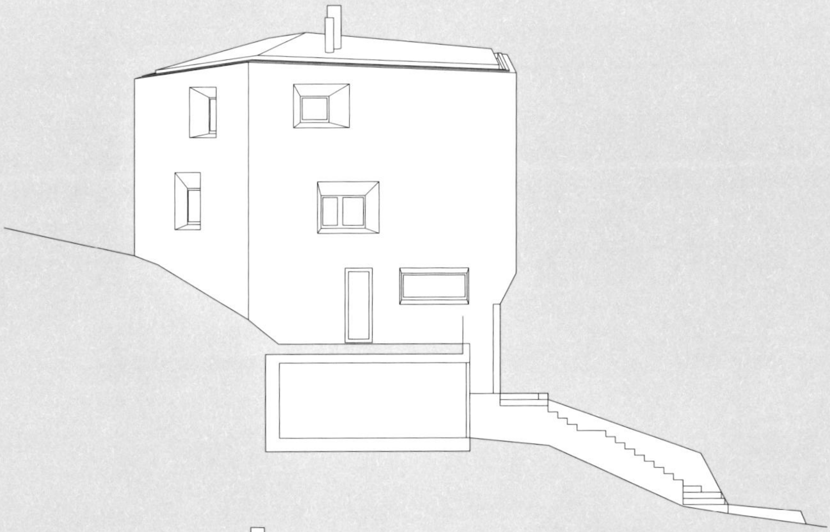

SOUTH

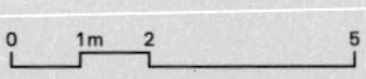

LONGITUDINAL SECTION A-A

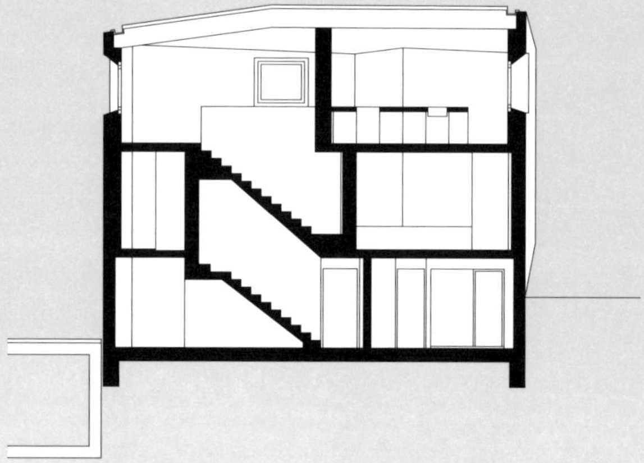

LONGITUDINAL SECTION B-B

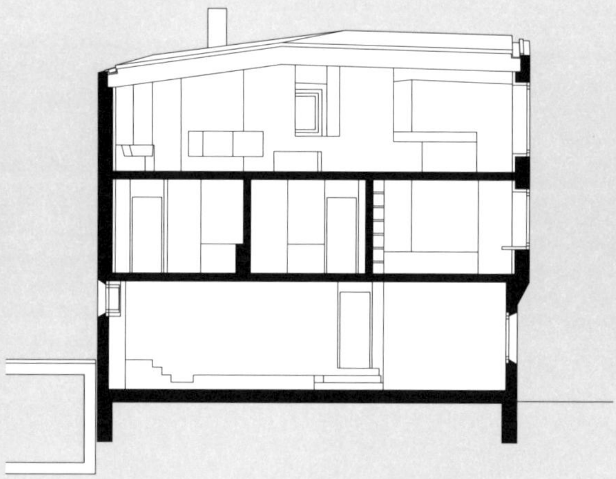

CROSS SECTION C-C

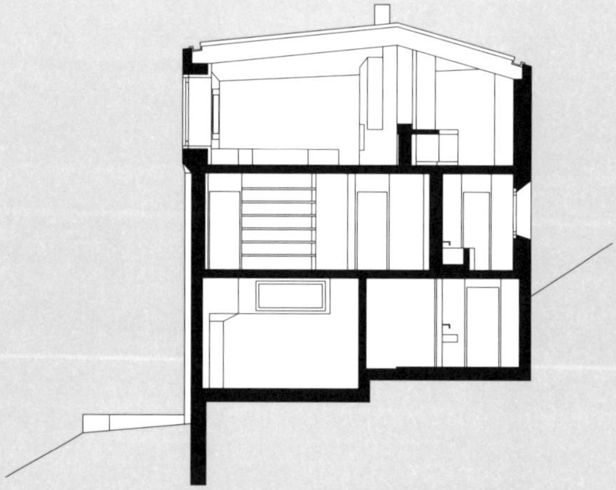

ROOF STORY

1 Dining / cooking
2 Living

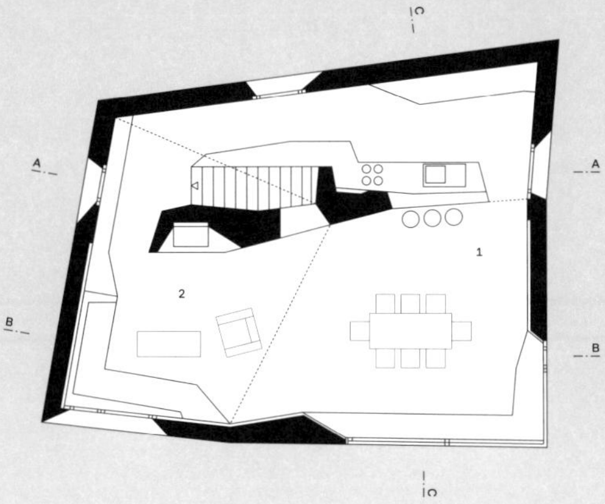

UPPER FLOOR

1 Guestroom
2 Sleeping
3 Dressing room
4 Bath / lavatory
5 Shower / lavatory

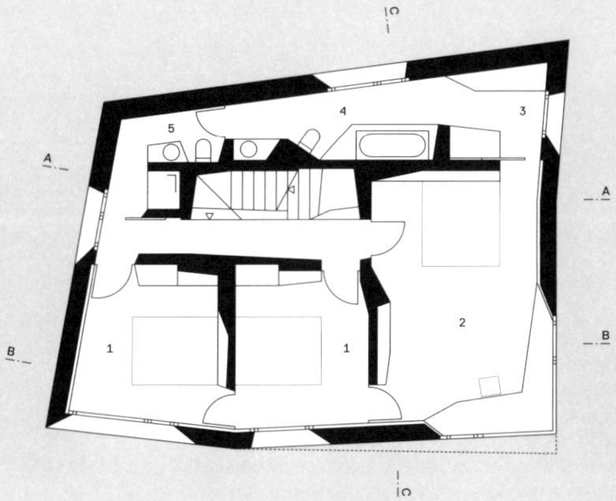

GROUND FLOOR

1 Entrance / gallery
2 Cellar
3 Shower / lavatory
4 Sauna
5 Service installations
6 Terrace

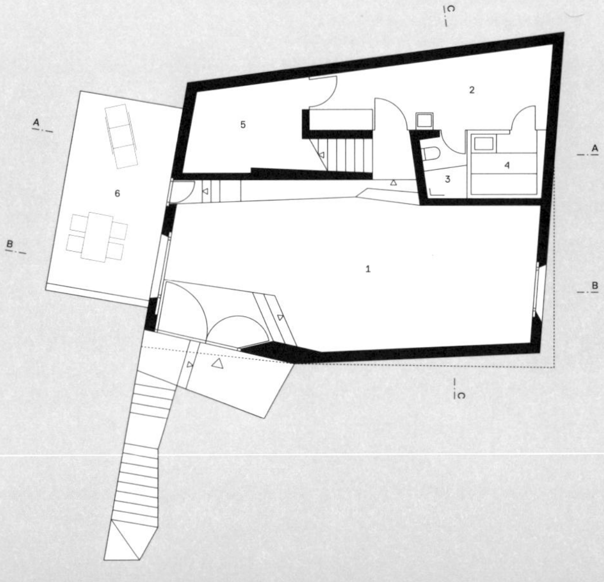

CEMETERY BUILDING 2007–2010

ERLENBACH

102 ↗

The siting of the new cemetery building architectonically brackets the cemetery grounds, directly on Lake Zurich, and the parallel position of the church, placing the two buildings in dialogue with each other and spanning the graveyards between them. As opposed to the church, this functionally hybrid building is conceived as a pavilion serving the secluded, intimate atmosphere of a cemetery. All the uses are combined within a free form situated under a massive, heavy roof. At the center are the rooms of the funeral chapel, which are accessed via a glazed corridor facing the cemetery. The green panes of glass, mostly opaque, serve as a visual barrier and form an important intermediate space for preparing to encounter the deceased. The walnut paneling and the natural overhead lighting give the funeral chapel an appropriate dignity, but also lend warmth and comfort. The introverted spaces provide the requisite silence for mourning and taking leave of the deceased.

The visitors' room and the covered exterior space, where small ceremonies can be held, are oriented towards the most beautiful point overlooking the lake. Two perforated, ornamental concrete walls in the covered outdoor area create a protective but solemn atmosphere.

The archaic-looking concrete construction contrasts pleasurably with the lightness of the glass façade, creating an abstract symbolism. The coloring of the glass panes in the façade, in various tones of green and brown, allows the pavilion to become part of the natural surroundings, and is related to the long tradition of applying colored glass to the sacred buildings within the most diverse cultures. The building's architectural expression is intended to help the mourners come to terms with the exceptional circumstances in which they find themselves, and to provide a dignified and contemporary setting for the mourning rituals of all confessions.

NORTHWEST

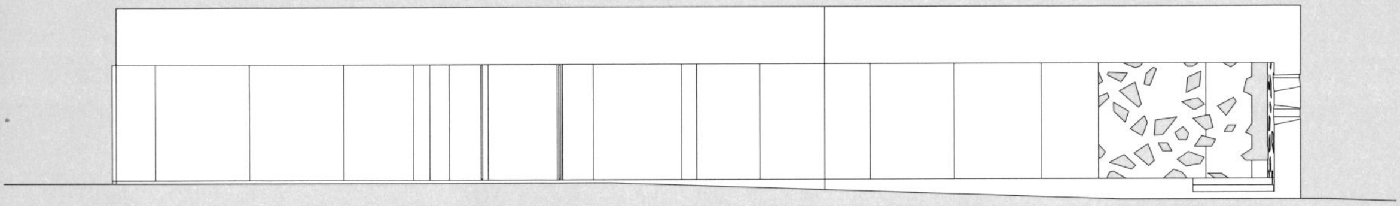

SOUTHEAST

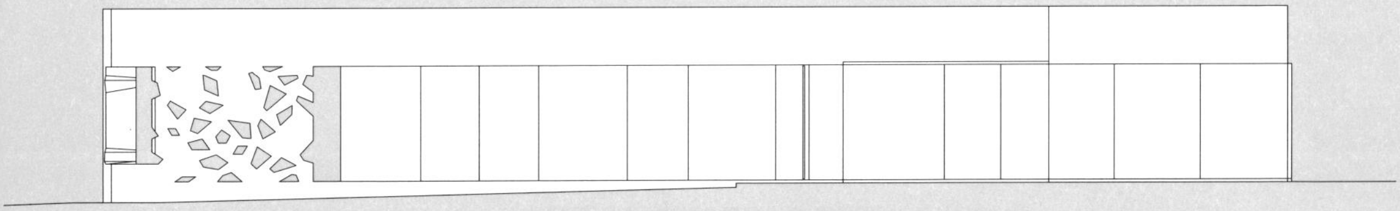

SOUTHWEST

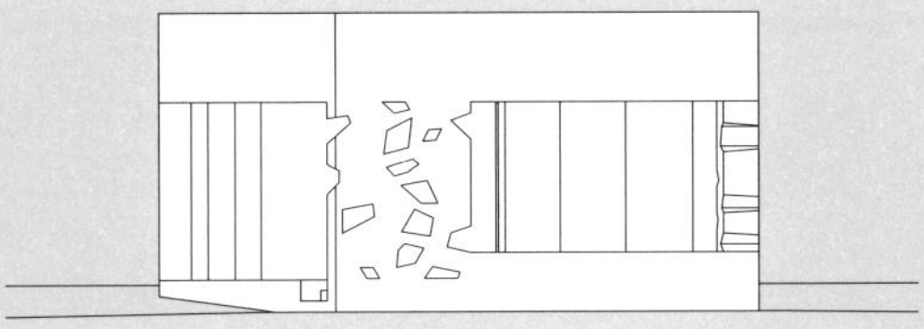

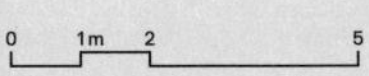

LONGITUDINAL SECTION A-A

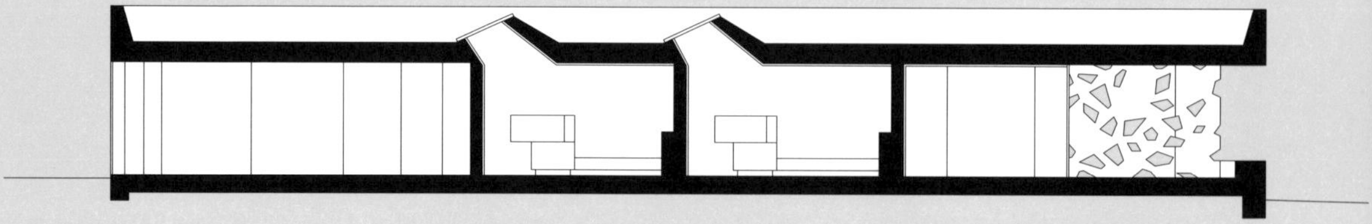

CROSS SECTION B-B

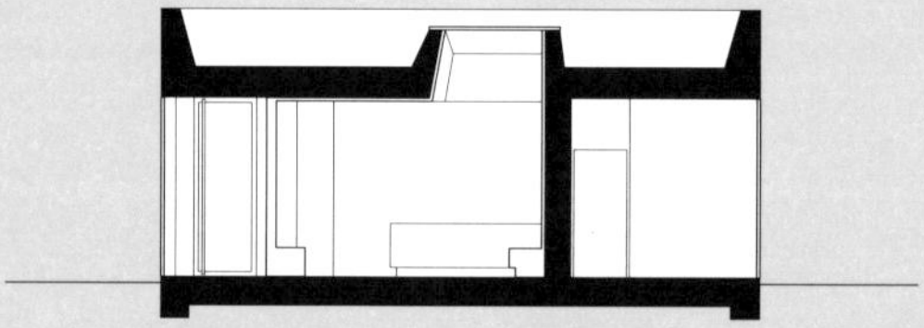

GROUND FLOOR

1 Covered vestibule
2 Visitor's room
3 Anteroom
4 Funeral parlor
5 Rear area
6 Gardener's room
7 Lavatory

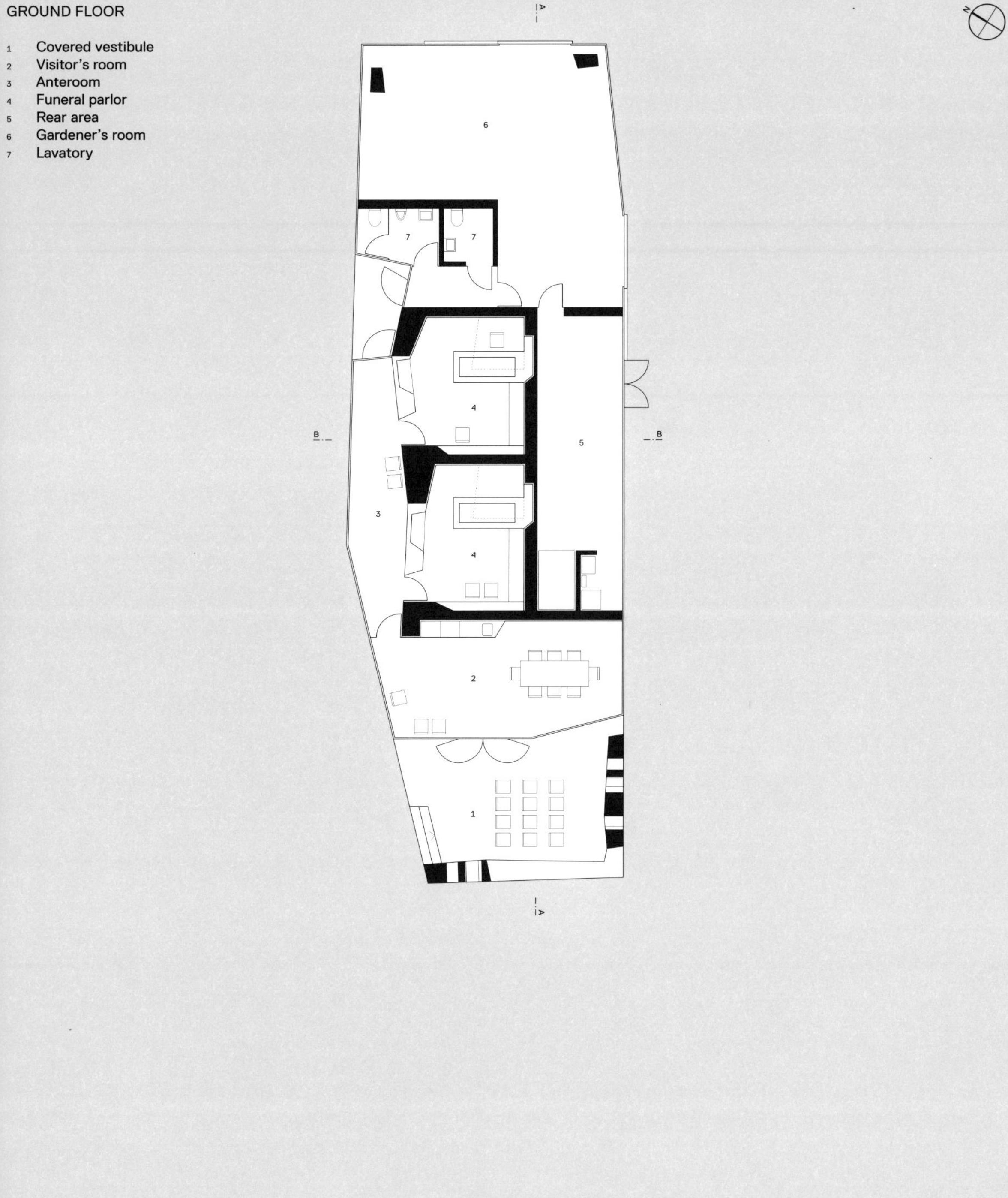

GABRIELLE HÄCHLER
ANDREAS FUHRIMANN

LIST OF WORKS
1988–2010

P	Projects
M	Furniture
A	Year
B	Project Title
C	Location
D	Client
E	Design
F	Collaboration

P1 PROJECT
A 1988
B Schöller site, Zurich
C Zurich
D Kunsthalle Zurich
E Andreas Fuhrimann
F Christian Karrer

P2 PROJECT
A 1989
B Canopies SCANIA
C Othmarsingen
D Hächler AG – SCANIA
E Gabrielle Hächler

P3 PROJECT
A 1989–1990
B Körfer Gugler House
C Rüschlikon, Zurich
D Thomas and Janine Körfer
E Andreas Fuhrimann
F Christian Karrer

P4 COMPETITION AND PROJECT
A 1989–1992
B Residential Development Münzlishausen
C Münzlishausen, Baden
D private clients' association
E Andreas Fuhrimann
F Christian Karrer

P5 PROJECT
A 1992
B Refurbishment Loft Apartment Kastanienbaum
C Kastanienbaum, Lucerne
D Thomas Steiger
E Gabrielle Hächler

P6 COMPETITION / 2ND PRIZE
A 1993
B Church Congregation Hall Hünenberg
C Hünenberg, Lucerne
D Hünenberg local authority
E Gabrielle Hächler
F Ivana Calovic

P7 PRELIMINARY PROJECT
A 1994
B Residential Development Binz
C Zurich
D Binz clients' association
E Andreas Fuhrimann

P8 PROJECT
A 1994
B Westdeutsche Landesbank Zurich
C Zurich
D Westdeutsche Landesbank
E Andreas Fuhrimann
F Christian Karrer

P9 PROJECT
A 1994–1996
B Schwob House
C Zurich
D Erika and Paul Schwob
E Gabrielle Hächler
F Nicole Woog

P10 PRELIMINARY STUDY
A 1995
B Development Railway Site Dübendorf
C Dübendorf, Zurich
D Municipality Dübendorf and SBB
E Andreas Fuhrimann
F Thomas Horvath

P11 PROJECT
A 1995–1996
B Kunsthalle Zurich Löwenbräu Factory
C Zurich
D Kunsthalle Zurich
E Andreas Fuhrimann
F Christian Karrer

P12 COMPETITION
A 1996
B Place of Contemplation
C Uri highway rest stop
D Canton Uri
E Andreas Fuhrimann

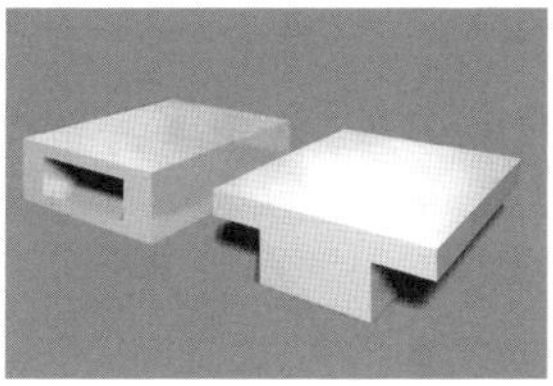

M1 CLUB TABLE
A 1996
C Conversion and Extension Flick
E AFGH
Andreas Fuhrimann,
Gabrielle Hächler

P13 COMPETITION
A 1997
B New Visual Identity
ETH Zurich
C Zurich
D ETH Zurich
E AFGH
Andreas Fuhrimann,
Gabrielle Hächler
F Pipilotti Rist, video artist
Trix Wetter and Irène Hiltpolt,
graphic designer

P14 PROJECT
A 1997
B Residential Workshop
Othmarsingen
C Othmarsingen
D Hächler AG
E AFGH
Andreas Fuhrimann,
Gabrielle Hächler

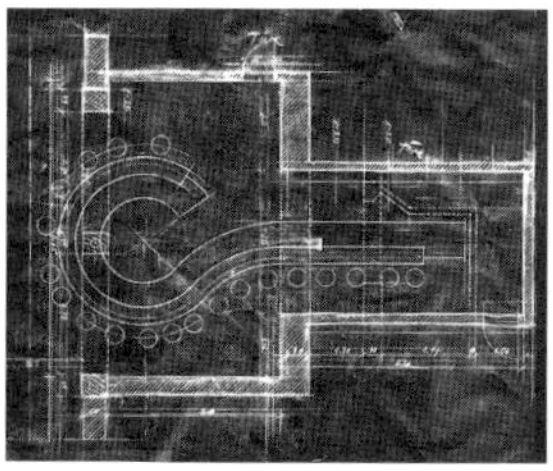

P15 PROJECT
A 1997
B Bar in Hotel Castell Zuoz
C Zuoz, Lower Engadine
D Ruedi Bechtler
E AFGH, Gabrielle Hächler
F Pipilotti Rist, video artist

P16 PROJECT
A 1997
B Conversion
Alpine Hut Blattistafel
C Gstaad area
D Friedrich Christian Flick
E AFGH
Andreas Fuhrimann,
Gabrielle Hächler

M2 BED
A 1997
C Conversion
Alpine Hut Blattistafel
E AFGH
Andreas Fuhrimann,
Gabrielle Hächler

M3 TABLE / CHESTS
A 1997
C Conversion
Alpine Hut Blattistafel
E AFGH
Andreas Fuhrimann,
Gabrielle Hächler

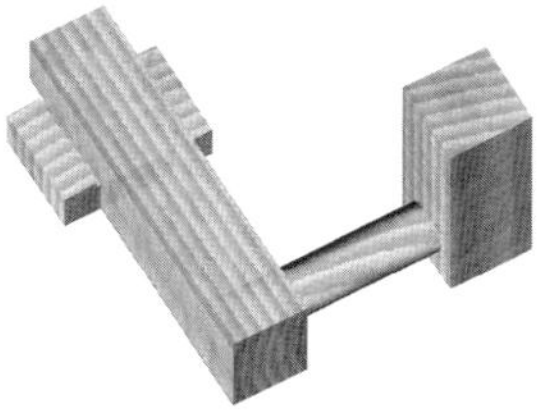

M4 DOOR HANDLE
A 1997
C Conversion
Alpine Hut Blattistafel
E AFGH
Andreas Fuhrimann,
Gabrielle Hächler

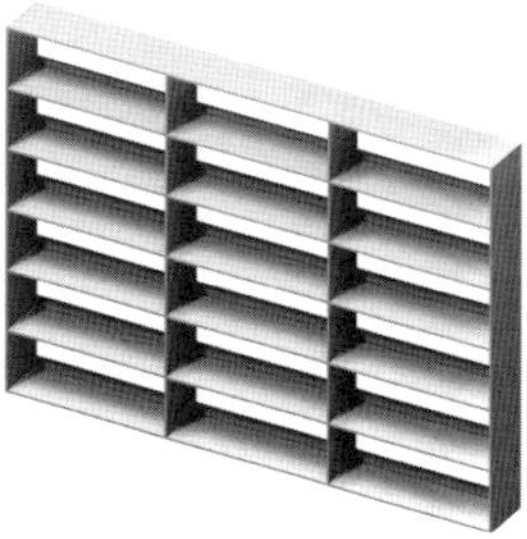

M5 ALUMINIUM SHELVING
A 1997
C Conversion
Alpine Hut Blattistafel
E AFGH
Andreas Fuhrimann,
Gabrielle Hächler

P17 STUDY
A 1998
B Apartment House Hotel Castell Zuoz
C Zuoz
D Ruedi Bechtler
E AFGH
Andreas Fuhrimann, Gabrielle Hächler, Urs Hüssy

P18 PROJECT
A 1998–1999
B Loft Peter Grünbaum and Office AFGH
C Zurich
D Peter Grünbaum
E AFGH
Andreas Fuhrimann, Gabrielle Hächler, Urs Hüssy

P19 PROJECT
A 1999
B Loft Susan Connor
C Zurich
D Susan Connor
E AFGH
Andreas Fuhrimann, Gabrielle Hächler, Urs Hüssy

M6 OFFICE-DESK COMBINATION
A 1999
C Office AFGH
E AFGH
Andreas Fuhrimann, Gabrielle Hächler

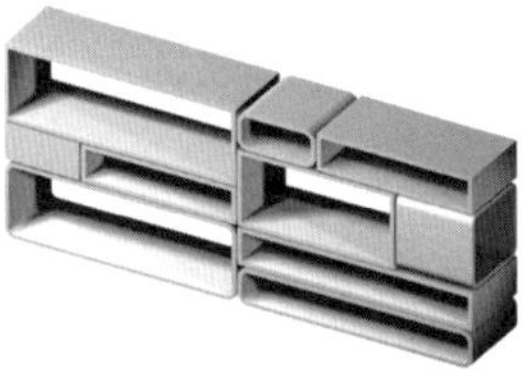

M7 MODULAR SHELVING
A 1999
C Office AFGH
E AFGH
Andreas Fuhrimann, Gabrielle Hächler

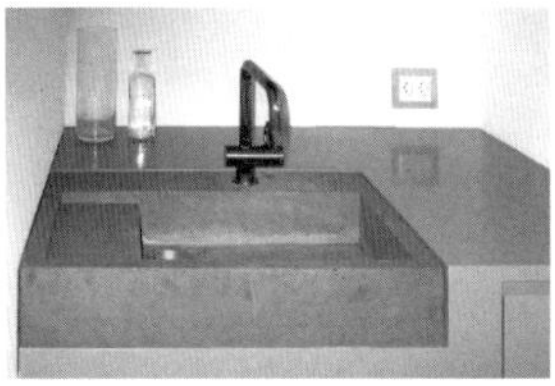

M8 WASH BASIN
A 1999
C Office AFGH
E AFGH
Andreas Fuhrimann, Gabrielle Hächler

M9 BATHTUB AND WASHSTAND
A 1999
C Loft Peter Grünbaum
E AFGH
Andreas Fuhrimann, Gabrielle Hächler

M10 TABLE
A 1999
C Loft Peter Grünbaum
E AFGH
Andreas Fuhrimann, Gabrielle Hächler

P20 COMPETITION
A 2000
B Extension National Museum
C Zurich
D Swiss Confederation
E AFGH
Andreas Fuhrimann, Gabrielle Hächler

P21 PROJECT
A 2000
B Art Space Zumikon
C Zumikon, Zurich
D J. and H. Hüssy
E AFGH
Andreas Fuhrimann, Gabrielle Hächler
F Urs Hüssy

M11 OFFICE DESK
A 2000
C Conversion and Extension Flick
E AFGH
Andreas Fuhrimann, Gabrielle Hächler

P22 COMPETITION / 2ND PRIZE
A 2001
B Visitor Center
Alptransit Gotthard
C Gotthard
D Alptransit Gotthard Inc.
E AFGH
Andreas Fuhrimann,
Gabrielle Hächler,
Urs Hüssy,
Manuel Arnold

P23 COMPETITION
A 2001
B Historisches Museum Bern
C Bern
D Foundation Historisches
Museum Bern
E AFGH
Andreas Fuhrimann,
Gabrielle Hächler,
Urs Hüssy

P24 STUDY ASSIGNMENT
A 2001
B Conversion and Extension
Kunstmuseum Basel
C Basel
D Kunstmuseum Basel
E AFGH
Andreas Fuhrimann,
Gabrielle Hächler,
Urs Hüssy

P25 COMPETITION AND PROJECT / 1ST PRIZE
A 2001–2003
B Riesbach Harbor Pavilion
C Zurich
D City of Zurich
E AFGH
Andreas Fuhrimann,
Gabrielle Hächler,
Ina Sperlich,
Barbara Schaub,
Carlo Fumarola

M12 DINING TABLE
A 2001
C Loft Peter Grünbaum
E AFGH
Andreas Fuhrimann,
Gabrielle Hächler

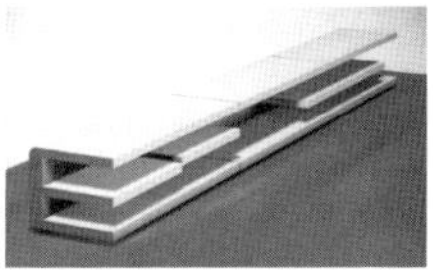

M13 SIDEBOARD
A 2001
C Loft Peter Grünbaum
E AFGH
Andreas Fuhrimann,
Gabrielle Hächler

M14 TABLES
A 2001
C Riesbach Harbor Pavilion
E AFGH
Andreas Fuhrimann,
Gabrielle Hächler

P26 PROJECT
A 2002
B Conversion and Extension Flick
C Gstaad
D Friedrich Christian Flick
E AFGH
Andreas Fuhrimann,
Gabrielle Hächler,
Andreas Maurer,
Thomas Frautschi

P27 STUDY
A 2002
B Nikon Switzerland
C Zurich
D Nikon Switzerland
E AFGH
Andreas Fuhrimann,
Gabrielle Hächler,
Urs Hüssy

P28 STUDY ASSIGNMENT
A 2002
B Weber House
C Weinfelden
D Ursula Weber
E AFGH
Andreas Fuhrimann,
Gabrielle Hächler

P29 PROJECT
A 2002–2003
B Architects' and Artists' House
on the Üetliberg
C Zurich
D Andreas Fuhrimann,
Gabrielle Hächler,
Pipilotti Rist, Balz Roth
E AFGH
Andreas Fuhrimann,
Gabrielle Hächler,
Ina Sperlich,
Carlo Fumarola

P30 COMPETITION
A 2003
B Residential Development A-Park
C Zurich
D City of Zurich
E AFGH
Andreas Fuhrimann,
Gabrielle Hächler,
Roland Heindl,
Ina Sperlich

P31 STUDY ASSIGNMENT
A 2003
B UNO GA Lobby
C New York
D Swiss Confederation
E AFGH
Andreas Fuhrimann,
Gabrielle Hächler,
Carlo Fumarola

M15 GARDEN TABLE
A 2003
C Architects' and Artists' House on the Üetliberg
E AFGH
Andreas Fuhrimann,
Gabrielle Hächler,
Barbara Schaub

P32 PROJECT
A 2003–2010
B Apartment House Röntgenstrasse
C Zurich
D STEG Röntgenstrasse
E AFGH
Andreas Fuhrimann,
Gabrielle Hächler,
Barbara Schaub,
Regula Zwicky

P33 PROJECT
A 2003–2004
B Holiday House on the Rigi
C Rigi-Scheidegg
D Andreas Fuhrimann,
Gabrielle Hächler,
Pius Sidler,
Victor Escobar
E AFGH
Andreas Fuhrimann,
Gabrielle Hächler,
Roland Heindl,
Carlo Fumarola

P34 COMPETITION
A 2004
B Auxiliary Buildings Zurich
C Zurich
D City of Zurich
E AFGH
Andreas Fuhrimann,
Gabrielle Hächler
F Thomas Horvath

P35 PROJECT
A 2004
B Loft Werenfels
C Zurich
D Stina Werenfels and Samir
E AFGH
Andreas Fuhrimann,
Gabrielle Hächler,
Barbara Schaub

P36 STUDY ASSIGNMENT
A 2004
B SBB-Viaduct Arches
C Zurich
D SBB and City of Zurich
E AFGH
Andreas Fuhrimann,
Gabrielle Hächler,
Marc Engler

M16 LECTERN
A 2004
C Hallen Stadium Zurich
E AFGH
Andreas Fuhrimann,
Gabrielle Hächler

M17 STACKABLE SIDEBOARD
A 2004
C Loft Presenhuber
E AFGH
Andreas Fuhrimann,
Gabrielle Hächler

M18 BED
A 2004
C Loft Presenhuber
E AFGH
Andreas Fuhrimann,
Gabrielle Hächler,
Barbara Schaub,
Manuel Frey

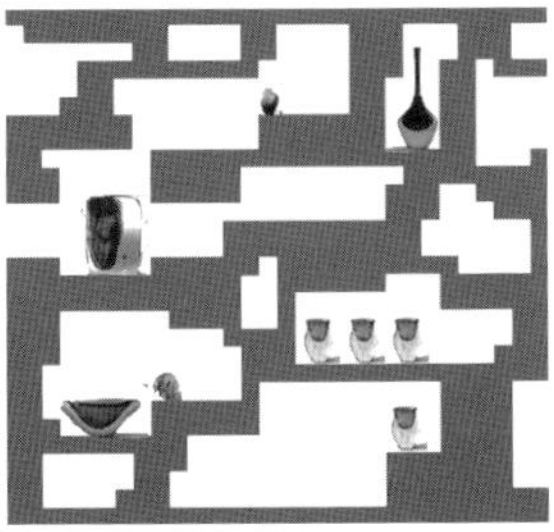

P37 PROJECT
A 2005
B Shop Refurbishment
1,000 Objects
C Zurich
D Peter Grünbaum
E AFGH
Andreas Fuhrimann,
Gabrielle Hächler,
Manuel Frey

P38 COMPETITION
A 2005
B Municipal Hospital Triemli
C Zurich
D City of Zurich
E AFGH
Andreas Fuhrimann,
Gabrielle Hächler,
Barbara Schaub,
Manuel Frey

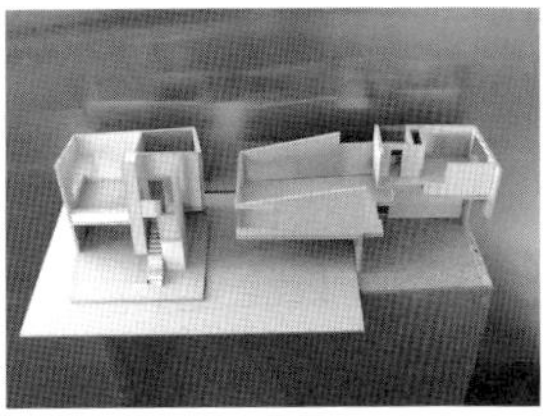

P39 PROJECT
A 2005–2007
B Müller Gritsch House
C Lenzburg
D Barbara Müller and
Stefan Gritsch
E AFGH
Andreas Fuhrimann,
Gabrielle Hächler,
Barbara Schaub,
Flavio Loretz

P40 COMPETITION
A 2005
B Residential Development Illnau
C Illnau-Effretikon
D SADA Pension Fund Inc.,
municipality Illnau-Effretikon
E AFGH
Andreas Fuhrimann,
Gabrielle Hächler
Barbara Schaub
F Sabine von Fischer

P41 PROJECT
A 2006
B Kitchen Installation
Marcel Breuer Villa
C Feldmeilen
D Maja Hoffmann
E AFGH
Andreas Fuhrimann,
Gabrielle Hächler

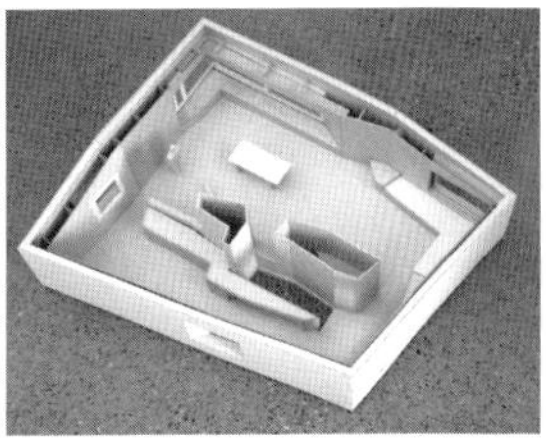

P42 PROJECT
A 2006–2007
B Presenhuber House
C Vnà
D Eva Presenhuber
E AFGH
Andreas Fuhrimann,
Gabrielle Hächler,
Barbara Schaub

P43 PROJECT
A 2006
B Conversion
Grieder Swarovski House
C Küsnacht
D Damian Grieder and
Melli Grieder-Swarovski
E AFGH
Andreas Fuhrimann,
Gabrielle Hächler,
Carlo Fumarola

P44 PROJECT
A 2006–2009
B Lanel Chalet
C Cordon (F)
D Isabelle and Denis Lanel
E AFGH
Andreas Fuhrimann,
Gabrielle Hächler,
Carlo Fumarola

P45 COMPETITION AND PROJECT
A 2006–2007
B Bar Haus Konstruktiv
C Zurich
D Foundation for Constructive
and Concrete Art
E AFGH
Andreas Fuhrimann,
Gabrielle Hächler,
Flavio Loretz,
Carlo Fumarola

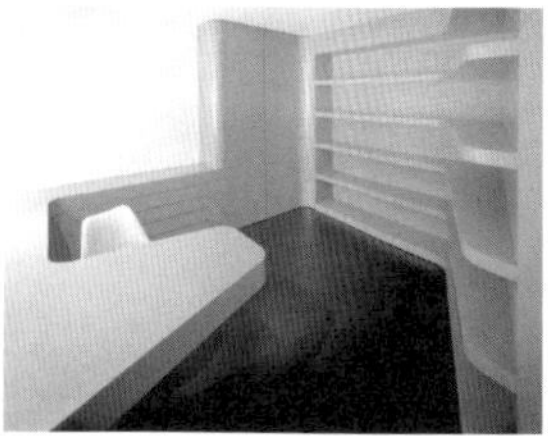

M19 OFFICE FURNITURE
A 2006
C Conversion
Grieder Swarovski House
E AFGH
Andreas Fuhrimann,
Gabrielle Hächler,
Carlo Fumarola

P46 PROJECT
A 2006–2010
B Alumnae Lounge
ETH Hönggerberg
C Zurich
D ETH Alumnae
E AFGH
Andreas Fuhrimann,
Gabrielle Hächler,
Manuel Frey,
Carlo Fumarola
F Roger Witzig
(preliminary project)

P47 PROJECT
A 2007–2010
B Conversion
Sonneur de Cloches
C Arles (F)
D Vera Michalski
E AFGH
Andreas Fuhrimann,
Gabrielle Hächler,
Regula Zwicky
F Max Romanet Architects,
Arles

P48 COMPETITION
A 2007
B Swiss Pavilion Expo 2010
C Shanghai
D Swiss Confederation
E AFGH
Andreas Fuhrimann,
Gabrielle Hächler,
Carlo Fumarola,
Barbara Schaub,
Regula Zwicky
F team stratenwerth

P49 COMPETITION AND PROJECT / 1ST PRIZE
A 2007–2010
B Cemetery Building Erlenbach
C Erlenbach
D Municipality Erlenbach
E AFGH
Andreas Fuhrimann,
Gabrielle Hächler,
Regula Zwicky,
Barbara Schaub,
Carlo Fumarola

P50 COMPETITION AND PROJECT / 1ST PRIZE
A 2007–2011
B Apartment Building Felsenburg
C Stäfa
D Regula und Peter Schuster
E AFGH
Andreas Fuhrimann,
Gabrielle Hächler,
F Barbara Schaub,
Marc Engler

P51 STUDY
A 2007
B Three Holiday Houses
C Reith in Alpnachtal (A)
D Gerhard Swarovski
E AFGH
Andreas Fuhrimann,
Gabrielle Hächler,
Marion Clauss,
Gilbert Isermann

P52 COMPETITION / 1ST PRIZE
A 2007
B Apartment Block Berlin
C Berlin
D Petur Arason,
Ragna Robertsdottir,
Karin Sander,
Bernhard Thome
E AFGH
Andreas Fuhrimann,
Gabrielle Hächler,
Flavio Loretz

P53 PROJECT
A 2008
B Conversion Chalet Ariel
C Gstaad
D Maja Hoffmann
E AFGH
Andreas Fuhrimann,
Gabrielle Hächler,
Barbara Schaub,
Carlo Fumarola

P54 PROJECT
A 2008–2009
B House in Central Switzerland
C Engelberg
D Felicitas Haack and
Alain Dutronc
E AFGH
Andreas Fuhrimann,
Gabrielle Hächler,
Gilbert Isermann

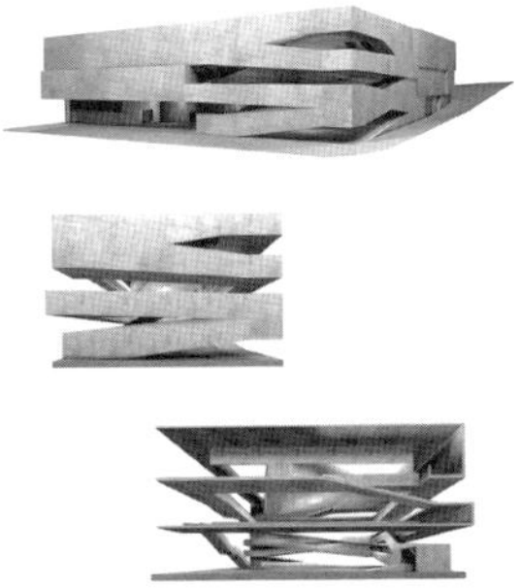

P55 COMPETITION
- A 2008
- B Extension Kunsthaus Zurich
- C Zurich
- D City of Zurich
- E AFGH
  Andreas Fuhrimann,
  Gabrielle Hächler,
  Marion Clauss,
  Carlo Fumarola,
  Gilbert Isermann,
  Hannes Reichel,
  Barbara Schaub,
  Regula Zwicky

P56 PROJECT
- A 2008–2011
- B Two Holiday Houses on Antiparos
- C Antiparos (GR)
- D Eva Presenhuber, Iasson Tsakonas
- E AFGH
  Andreas Fuhrimann,
  Gabrielle Hächler,
  Manuel Frey,
  Regula Zwicky,
  Carlo Fumarola,
  Marion Clauss

P57 PROJECT
- A 2008–2011
- B Kux House
- C Küsnacht
- D Barbara Kux and Marc Parein
- E AFGH
  Andreas Fuhrimann,
  Gabrielle Hächler,
  Marion Clauss

P58 PROJECT
- A 2008–2011
- B House in Rüti
- C Rüti
- D Cécile Graf and Walter Gloor
- E AFGH
  Andreas Fuhrimann,
  Gabrielle Hächler,
  Barbara Schaub

P59 PRELIMINARY PROJECT
- A 2008
- B Good House
- C Sargans
- D Jörg Good
- E AFGH
  Andreas Fuhrimann,
  Gabrielle Hächler,
  Regula Zwicky

P60 STUDY ASSSIGNMENT
- A 2008
- B Art 40 Basel
- C Basel
- D Art Basel
- E AFGH
  Andreas Fuhrimann,
  Gabrielle Hächler,
  Maud Cassaignau

P61 PROJECT
- A 2008–2009
- B Ludobox
- C Gstaad
- D Maja Hoffmann
- E AFGH
  Andreas Fuhrimann,
  Gabrielle Hächler,
  Carlo Fumarola,
  Gilbert Isermann

P62 PROJECT
- A 2008–2011
- B Gallery Presenhuber Maag Site
- C Zurich
- D Eva Presenhuber
- E AFGH
  Andreas Fuhrimann,
  Gabrielle Hächler,
  Gilbert Isermann

M20 SOFA
A 2008
C Conversion Chalet Ariel
E AFGH
Andreas Fuhrimann,
Gabrielle Hächler,
Carlo Fumarola

M21 BED
A 2008
C Presenhuber House
E AFGH
Andreas Fuhrimann,
Gabrielle Hächler,
Barbara Schaub

P63 STUDY ASSIGNMENT
A 2009–2012
B Apartment Houses Hungerberg
C Aarau
D Pierre Rothpletz
E AFGH
Andreas Fuhrimann,
Gabrielle Hächler,
Gilbert Isermann,
Manuel Frey,
Marion Clauss
F Lars Müller

P64 STUDY
A 2009–2010
B Two Holiday Houses
Suvrettahang
C St. Moritz
D Marcella and
Hans Peter Bauer
E AFGH
Andreas Fuhrimann,
Gabrielle Hächler,
Marion Clauss

P65 STUDY ASSIGNMENT AND PROJECT
A 2009–
B CIVIS
C global
D Citadel Development
Corporation Ltd.
E AFGH
Andreas Fuhrimann,
Gabrielle Hächler,
Carlo Fumarola

P66 COMPETITION
A 2009
B Cultural Center
Les Arts Gstaad
C Gstaad
D Foundation Les Arts Gstaad
E AFGH
Andreas Fuhrimann,
Gabrielle Hächler,
Marion Clauss,
Carlo Fumarola,
Manuel Frey,
Gilbert Isermann,
Barbara Schaub,
Regula Zwicky

P67 COMPETITION AND REVISION
A 2009–2010
B Apartment Building
Hottingerplatz
C Zurich
D Family Waeber and
Tobias Frey
E AFGH
Andreas Fuhrimann,
Gabrielle Hächler,
Marion Clauss,
Carlo Fumarola,
Manuel Frey,
Gilbert Isermann,
Barbara Schaub,
Regula Zwicky

P68 PROJECT
A 2009–2010
B Conversion
Doswald Strauss House
C Hinterbuchenegg, Zurich
D Christoph Doswald and
Dorothea Strauss
E AFGH
Andreas Fuhrimann,
Gabrielle Hächler,
Nicola Baviera

M22 NIGHTSTAND
A 2009
C Holiday House on the Rigi
E AFGH
Andreas Fuhrimann,
Gabrielle Hächler,
Flavio Loretz

P69 PROJECT
A 2010–2011
B Rondinone House
C Würenlos
D Ugo Rondinone
E AFGH
Andreas Fuhrimann,
Gabrielle Hächler,
Gilbert Isermann,
Barbara Schaub

P70 PROJECT
A 2010–2012
B Farm Bärgiswil
C Küssnacht
D Susanne Frei-Kleiner and Hans T. Frei
E AFGH
Andreas Fuhrimann,
Gabrielle Hächler,
Barbara Schaub

P71 PROJECT
A 2010–2012
B Schepers House
C Küsnacht
D Martina and Gerd Schepers
E AFGH
Andreas Fuhrimann,
Gabrielle Hächler,
Carlo Fumarola

M23 SOFA
A 2010
C Ludobox
E AFGH
Andreas Fuhrimann,
Gabrielle Hächler,
Carlo Fumarola

M24 SIDEBOARD
A 2010
C Conversion
Doswald Strauss House
E AFGH
Andreas Fuhrimann,
Gabrielle Hächler

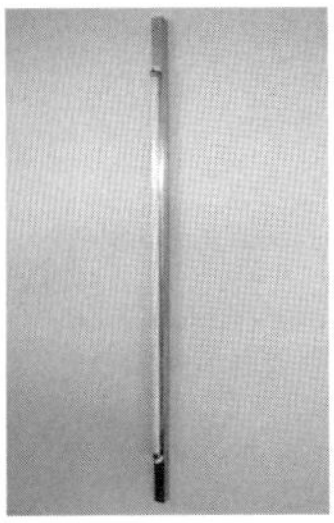

M25 LIGHT
A 2010
C Apartment House
Röntgenstrasse
E AFGH
Andreas Fuhrimann,
Gabrielle Hächler,
Regula Zwicky
F AA Arber Agency,
Florian Arber

P72 EXHIBITION
A 2010
C AFGH exhibition, ETH Zurich
E AFGH
Andreas Fuhrimann,
Gabrielle Hächler,
Manuel Frey,
Regula Zwicky
F gta Institute, ETH Zurich

BIOGRAPHIES

HUBERTUS ADAM

Studied art history, archaeology, and philosophy at the University of Heidelberg. Since 1991, freelance architecture critic for the *Neue Zürcher Zeitung*. From 1996 to 1997, editor for *Bauwelt* in Berlin. Since 1998, editor of *archithese* in Zurich. Numerous book publications and articles, in addition to activities as chairman, speaker, and jury member. Swiss Art Award for art and architecture communication, 2004. Since 2010, art director at the Swiss Architecture Museum (SAM) in Basel.

KURT W. FORSTER

Lectured at various American universities (Yale, Stanford, MIT). From 1975 to 1977, director of the Swiss Institute, Rome; 1984–1993, founding director of the Getty Research Institute in Los Angeles; 1999–2001, director of the Canadian Center for Architecture in Montreal; and director of the Architecture Biennale Venice, 2004. From 1992 to 1999, he lectured at ETH Zurich and is currently visiting professor at the Yale School of Architecture. He has realized exhibitions of Schinkel's stage-scenery designs (Chicago, 1994) and the works of Carlo Scarpa (Vicenza and Verona, 2000) and Herzog & de Meuron (Montreal, 2002). He holds the title of Accademico di San Luca and is a member of the Consiglio Scientifico at the Centro Internazionale di Studi di Architettura Andrea Palladio in Vicenza. In 2009, he was awarded the Meret Oppenheim Prize.

GIANNI JETZER

Studied art history, modern history, and media studies at the University of Zurich. From 1998 to 2001, curator at the Migros Museum in Zurich; 2001–2006, director of the Kunsthalle St. Gallen; since 2006, director of the Swiss Institute, New York. Numerous exhibitions as a freelance curator (including for *curated by_vienna* and the Museum Tinguely in Basel). Art critic (including for *Parkett*, *Flash Art*, *Neue Zürcher Zeitung*) and author. Since 2009, permanent visiting lectureship at Zurich University of the Arts (ZHdK).

MARIE THERES STAUFFER

Studied architecture, art history, philosophy, and modern German literature. From 1997 to 2000, academic assistant at the ETH Zurich; 2000–2002, visiting fellow at the Kunsthistorisches Institut in Florenz. In 2002, received doctorate title from the University of Zurich. From 2002 to 2003, post-doctoral fellowship at the Bibliotheca Hertziana, Max Planck Institute for Art History, Rome; 2003–2008, research associate at the Institute of Art History, University of Zurich; 2008–2009, academic assistant at the Karman Center, University of Bern; 2008–2009, Alexander von Humboldt fellow at Humbolt Üniversität zu Berlin. From 2009 to 2010 visiting professorship at the University of Konstanz. Since 2010, Swiss National Science Foundation (SNF) research professor at the Unité d'histoire de l'Art, University of Geneva.